The Battle of Bannockburn.

*Printed by R Clark*
FOR
EDMONSTON & DOUGLAS, EDINBURGH

| | |
|---|---|
| LONDON . | HAMILTON, ADAMS, AND CO |
| CAMBRIDGE | MACMILLAN AND CO |
| GLASGOW | JAMES MACLEHOSE |

# A HISTORY

OF THE

# Battle of Bannockburn

FOUGHT A.D. 1314,

WITH

NOTICES OF THE PRINCIPAL WARRIORS WHO
ENGAGED IN THAT CONFLICT

BY

ROBERT WHITE

AUTHOR OF A 'HISTORY OF THE BATTLE OF OTTERBURN,' 'POEMS,' ETC.

> Although our honoured patriots sleep in dust,
> The glory they achieved we now enjoy;
> Then let us venerate their very names,
> And gaze upon the soil as hallowed ground
> Whereon they fought and conquered!

**With Map and Armorial Bearings**

EDINBURGH
EDMONSTON AND DOUGLAS
MDCCCLXXI

TO EVERY TRUE SCOTSMAN,

RICH OR POOR,

WHOSE ANCESTORS MAY HAVE FOUGHT WITH

THE BRUCE AT BANNOCKBURN,

AND WHOSE HEART GLOWS WITH PATRIOTISM

AS HE PONDERS

OVER THE FREEDOM AND INDEPENDENCE ACHIEVED

FOR THEIR COUNTRY BY

THE WARRIORS OF SCOTLAND

ON THAT MEMORABLE BATTLE-FIELD,

THIS VOLUME

IS RESPECTFULLY DEDICATED BY

THE AUTHOR.

# PREFACE.

BEING born on the Scottish Border, and hearing from my parents' lips of The Bruce and The Douglas, and of the battles of Bannockburn and Otterburn, I desired, as I grew up, to know something of the lives of these men, and to wander over the localities whereon they led their armies to victory. In this way, when I came to reflect on the privileges which Scotland derived from the former of these battle-fields, the place came to be regarded by me as hallowed ground, and The Bruce I accounted, next to Wallace, the bravest warrior that ever drew the sword in defence of that country, besides being the greatest monarch that ever sat upon her throne.

Having, therefore, by the divine blessing, arrived at a period of existence when, in a great measure, I had overcome the toil and trouble of active life, I turned my attention to the history of Scotland during the early part of the fourteenth century, comprising the ascendency of Bruce, and, after no inconsiderable amount of research, the present volume is the result of my investigation. Exercising my own judgment among the numerous authorities I consulted, and being desirous, above every other consideration, of ascertaining what must actually have taken place at Bannockburn, my dependence has been placed chiefly on the 'Metrical History of Robert the First, King of Scotland, by John Barbour, Archdeacon of Aberdeen;' and my reason for relying on that author is, that he lived at a time when the actions he enumerates were related to him by the common people, many of whom had witnessed and borne a share in their fulfilment. Allan de Cathcart told him he was present when Edward Bruce defeated the forces of Sir Ingram de Umfreville and Sir John de Saint John in Galloway, six years before the battle of Bannockburn was fought.[1] Hence he had both seen and conversed with those who had espoused the cause of Bruce, and supported that hero in his onward course till the freedom of Scotland was consummated. Indeed, as I have on several occasions carefully examined the whole of the ground on the field and around it, and bestowed ample consideration on every contingency connected with the event, the impression on my mind is more and more confirmed that, in company with one or more intelligent men who were engaged in that battle, and knew every movement thereof, Barbour himself had traversed the whole locality more than once, and had the several spots pointed out to him where the main onslaughts were made, and where the particular incidents, both before and after the conflict, took place. The arrangement of the forces, both of England and Scotland, as narrated by him, with their several evolutions, harmonises in a remarkable degree with the undulation of the ground, and warrants the conclusion that the venerable

---

[1] *Barbour*, p. 183.

old chronicler had spared no pains honestly and fairly to write out, so far as he was enabled, an accurate account of the great battle, and to glean all he could learn of the life and actions of the Bruce.

Still, though placing great reliance on the various statements of Barbour, I do not consider him in every point perfect, nor have I hesitated to differ from him when he relates what, in my opinion, will not bear the test of calm deliberate judgment. My aim has been to discard improbability, and search for truth in whatever form it may be ascertained. Every individual who presumes to write history ought to sift the evidence most carefully which he has amassed before him, and endeavour, so far as his power of discrimination will enable him, to separate what is correct from that which, under any form, may appear doubtful. Unfortunately, we have perceived, time after time, that when one historian stoops to follow another implicitly, without the exercise of his higher powers, we have the same error repeated over and over again. This ought no longer to be tolerated.

Another author to whom I have been indebted, is Robert Kerr, in his 'History of Scotland during the reign of Robert First, surnamed the Bruce.' Like the 'Border History' by Ridpath, his work is by no means attractive to the general reader, yet the research and labour these compilations must have cost their authors deserve cordial acknowledgment. Other collateral sources, as may be seen by the imposing list of authorities hereafter annexed, I have diligently explored. From recent historians I have drawn little, their statements being of slight value; and, not caring to solicit assistance from contemporary individuals whose knowledge of the early history of our country may be superior to my own, I set myself to work steadily on the subject I had selected to elucidate, and now hope that my effort may not altogether be in vain. No public event ever took place in Scotland that tended so effectually to form and exalt the national character of her sons as the victory over aggression that our ancestors won at Bannockburn. The self-dependence thereby established, which at the close of last century was still more awakened into activity by the strains of Robert Burns, has made that region what she is—a realm renowned over the world for the loyalty, the morality, the trustworthiness, and the ennobling virtues of her people. Nor is it without some degree of pleasurable feeling that the author places this volume before the public, in the assurance that he thereby contributes his mite towards the illustration of a most important part of the history of his native land.

The map has been carefully corrected and engraved from that of the Board of Ordnance by Messrs. Johnston of Edinburgh. The shields which accompany the Biographical Notices were cut by Mr. John Cleghorn of London, to whose skill and ability the author was indebted for those which embellish the memoirs of the warriors who figure in his 'History of the Battle of Otterburn.'

R. W.

11 CLAREMONT PLACE,
NEWCASTLE-UPON-TYNE, *23d September* 1871.

## A BRIEF NOTICE OF

# John Barbour,

#### AUTHOR OF 'THE BRUCE.'

We have no authentic account either when or where John Barbour was born, but the date of his birth is supposed to be from about 1318 down to the period near the death of Robert Bruce, which took place in 1329. He appears, notwithstanding the meaning of his name, to have been of a respectable family, for, entering the church, he was in 1356 promoted to the Archdeaconry of Aberdeen. Being desirous of mental cultivation, even in middle age, and unable to find suitable teachers in his own land, he obtained in 1357 a safe conduct from Edward the Third to go to Oxford, with three scholars in his company. In the same year he was named, by the bishop of his diocese, one of three proxies to attend the important national council at Edinburgh, that funds might be voted for the ransom of David the Second, who had been made prisoner at the battle of Neville's Cross. Again he left Scotland in 1364, having obtained a safe conduct for himself and four horsemen to pass to Oxford or elsewhere, as he might deem proper. Also, in the following year, he was allowed to pass through England, with six persons in his company, on his way to St. Denis, near to Paris; and again, in 1368, King Edward granted letters of safe conduct to him, with two servants and two horses, to pass through his dominions towards France. These several excursions would appear to have been undertaken with the design of pursuing his studies in the universities both of England and the Continent.

On his return to Scotland after these pilgrimages in quest of learning, he would seem to have been much employed in the public service.  At that time scarcely any of the people, whether high or low, could even read or write, and possessing little or no knowledge of figures, any office connected with the public accounts usually devolved upon the clergy, who had undergone, less or more, a course of education, by which they became qualified for that duty.  Barbour in this way was appointed in 1373 Clerk of Audit of the King's Household, and also one of the Auditors of the Exchequer, then sitting at Perth.  Afterwards, in 1375, he was occupied, he tells us, in compiling his great work on *The Bruce*, which in all likelihood would occupy two or three years of his time.[1] On completing the book he was likely a sharer in the Royal bounty, for the Exchequer account in 1377 allows to the Receivers of Customs at Aberdeen ten pounds, paid to the bard by order of the King  In the following year he had another gift from the Sovereign of twenty shillings yearly out of the farms of Aberdeen for ever, with power to assign.  He had also in 1381 a gift from the crown of the ward of a minor, whose estate was within his parish.  And, moreover, in 1388, Robert the Second granted to John Barbour, yearly, for his life, the sum of ten pounds sterling out of the great customs of Aberdeen.  In addition to this, and the revenue of his prebend, which comprised the tithes and dues of the parish of Rayne in the Garioch, he had a considerable income from his office of Archdeacon.  The annuity of ten pounds was paid to him for seven years, and thence at the close, we learn the period of his decease, which occurred from Martinmas 1394 to Whitsunday 1395  Probably the day on which he died was the 13th of March, for afterwards on that day, yearly, an anniversary was celebrated in the Cathedral, down to the time of the Reformation, for the soul of Master John Barbour, sometime Archdeacon of Aberdeen

---

[1] Gawin Douglas completed the translation of 'Virgil's Æneis' into Scottish verse in about sixteen or eighteen months, immediately before the Battle of Flodden, in 1513.  Again, John Rolland of Dalkeith, in 1560, translated also into Scottish metre 'The Seven Sages,' in the course of seven weeks, which was published at Edinburgh in 1578  A reprint was issued in 1837, in black letter, by the Bannatyne Club  It is a quarto volume of about 360 pages

## LIFE OF BARBOUR.

Such endowments, taken altogether, must have made the venerable poetical chronicler very comfortable during the later years of his pilgrimage on earth. Fortunately he lived at the very time when he could collect from living men all the information which existed in Scotland relative to 'The Bruce,' and on his several journeyings to England we may be certain that he often passed the Forth at Stirling, and was familiar with all the remarkable places in that vicinity. His acquaintance with the people of Scotland of every class was no doubt extensive, and his industry in gleaning all they could tell him of his favourite hero is proved by the valuable record he has left us, which will ever remain an enduring monument of his fame.

From recent investigations we have proof that John Barbour tried his hand on other works than the one for which he has been so justly celebrated. The deserving editors who labour for *The Early English Text Society* intend to place in the hands of subscribers two publications written by the author of 'The Bruce,' the manuscripts of which were discovered in the University Library of Cambridge, by Mr. Henry Bradshaw, the librarian. One is composed of portions of a verse 'Troy Book,' and the other consists of the 'Lives of Saints,' in the northern dialect, also in verse, but of very considerable length.

The following extract, relative to *Barbour* and 'The Bruce,' is from the pen of Frederick J. Furnivall, Esq., an honest and indefatigable worker in opening up the treasures of our early British literature. It appears in his latest contribution to the *Ballad Society*, entitled 'Captain Cox, his Ballads and Books,' p. cxlii., 1871, and is brief, pointed, and comprehensive :—

'No printed edition before about 1570 is now known. Only two MSS. of the poem are known, of which the best, which has lost its first third, is in the Library of St. John's College, Cambridge, and is dated 1487. The inferior MS. is in the Advocates' Library, Edinburgh; is complete; is dated 1489; was edited by Dr. Jamieson in 1820, and reprinted at Glasgow, with all its mistakes, in 1869. The Rev. W. W. Skeat is now re-editing the work, from both MSS. and the old printed editions, for *The Early English Text Society's* extra series. Part I. was published in 1870. Mr. Cosmo Innes made a dreadful mess of the text, which he symmetrised, in his edition for the Spalding Club, 1856.'

Moreover, John Pinkerton published in London, 1790, an

edition of the work from the Edinburgh MS, in three volumes. On the supposition that Jamieson's copy was probably more correct, the author, having no more reliable source, was induced to select his extracts from the Quarto of 1820, as corroborative evidence of the correctness of the text in this volume. It may form a subject for consideration if an edition of 'The Bruce,' might still be published, embodying all the contractions and points which appear on the originals, taking the Edinburgh MS to complete, at the commencement, what is wanting in that of Cambridge, and then adopting the latter onward to the conclusion. We would then have all we can hope to glean of the venerable Archdeacon's Metrical History of The Bruce of Bannockburn.

# CONTENTS.

## CHAPTER I.

### PRELIMINARY OBSERVATIONS.

Aggressive movements of Edward I., 1—Scotland covered with forests, 3—Arms and implements imported, 5—Equipment of Men for War, 6—English Knights and Men-at-arms deemed invincible, 9—Spearmen obtain victory at Courtray, and importance thereof to Bruce, 10.

## CHAPTER II.

### MUSTERING OF FORCES.

Bruce recognised by the Three Estates in Scotland as lawful King, 12—Intention of John de Menteith to capture the Bruce, 13—Scots aware of the value of Freedom, 14—Edward Bruce besieges the Castle of Stirling, 15—Mowbray stipulates to surrender it in a stated period, 16—King Edward's exertions to retain his ascendency in Scotland, 17—He arrives at Newminster Abbey, 19—Scots stand true to their King and Country, 21—King Edward enters Scotland, 22.

## CHAPTER III.

### LOCALITIES NEAR THE BATTLE-FIELD.

Numbers of the Army of England, 25—Camp-followers and carriages, etc., 28—Intention of the English to capture and appropriate Scotland, 29—Wisdom of Bruce in selecting Bannockmoor as the field of battle, 30—Strength of the Castle of Stirling, 32—Halbert's Bog and Milton Bog, 33—Bruce's design to compel the English to meet his Army face to face, 35—He intends the enemy shall be crowded together, that the wings thereof may not be extended, 36.

## CHAPTER IV.

### ADVANCE OF THE SCOTS TO NEW PARK.

Robert Bruce examines his Army, 37—Communicates to his chief Men his arrangement for battle, 39—The Army separated into Four Divisions, 40—That under Bruce to form the rearward, 42—The whole move forward on the Roman road to Bannockmoor, *ib.*—Pits dug at Milton, 43—Position of the Scottish Army, 45.

## CHAPTER V.

### COMMENCEMENT OF HOSTILITIES.

The Scottish Army hears mass, 46—Bruce examines the pits and approves of them, 47—Proclamation made that such as dreaded the conflict had full liberty to go home, 48—Departure of Camp-followers to Gillies Hill, 50—Randolph charged to prevent the English passing to Stirling, *ib*—Douglas and Keith sent to observe the approach of the Enemy, 51—A Troop of English horse under Clifford departs to relieve Stirling Castle, 53—It is observed by Bruce, 54—Randolph pursues them, 55—Engages Clifford's Cavalry, 56

## CHAPTER VI

### DEATH OF DE BOHUN

Bruce occupies the Field with his Army, 60—Onward movement of the English, 61—Bruce attacked by Sir Henry Bohun, whom he kills with his battle-axe, 62—Scottish Chiefs blame him for his high sense of honour, 63—Clifford and his horsemen defeated, 64—Cordial welcome awarded to Randolph, 65—Bruce admonishes his Army, and his chief Men desire to be placed in order of Battle, 66

## CHAPTER VII

### PREPARATION FOR BATTLE.

Bruce addresses his warriors, 67-71—They all agree to his orders, 72—Relic of the Arm of Saint Fillan, *ib*—Anxiety of Robert Bruce, 73—Incident of Two Knights of Brabant, *ib.*—The English much discomforted, 74—They retire to rest, 75—Revelry in the English Camp, 76

## CHAPTER VIII.

### ARMIES OPPOSE EACH OTHER.

Bruce draws up his Forces for battle, 77—Knighthood conferred on several Scottish Leaders, 78—Detachments stationed at outposts, 79—Edward Bruce leads the van, *ib*—Randolph heads the Second Division, 80—The Steward and Douglas command the Third, *ib*—Bruce holds the Fourth in Reserve, *ib*—Imposing appearance of Both Armies. 81-2—King Edward inquires of Umfreville anent the Scots, 83-4—The Abbot of Inchaffray admonishes his Countrymen, 85—English Trumpet sounds the onset, 86.

## CHAPTER IX.

### THE BATTLE COMMENCES.

English Cavalry attack the van of the Scots, 89—This foreseen by Bruce, 90—English Archers pour their shafts upon their opponents, 91—Scots maintain in front an unbroken Line, 92—The Steward and Douglas next assailed, 93—Bruce sends Keith to attack the English Archers, 95—They are totally dispersed, 96—The Division under Bruce moves forward, and the battle is most fiercely fought, 97.

## CHAPTER X.

### BATTLE CONTINUED.

Whole Forces of Scotland engaged in Battle, 99—Scottish front moves onward over every obstacle, 100—Barbour soars into the region of poetry on describing the scene, 101—Scots still preserve uniformity in their front Lines, 103—Camp-followers move down from Gillies Hill, 104—Immense slaughter of the English, 105—Earl of Gloucester slain, and the Scots press on to victory, 106.

## CHAPTER XI.

### FLIGHT OF THE ENGLISH.

Agonising thoughts of the English King, 108—Death of Sir Giles de Argentine, 109—King Edward rides to Stirling Castle, 110—Departs on the road towards Linlithgow, 111—Abundant booty seized by the Scots, 112—Earl of Hereford escapes to Bothwell Castle, 114—Numbers of English retreat to the rocks at Stirling Castle, 115—Flight of King Edward, 116—He is received into the Castle of Dunbar, 117—Escapes by sea to England, 118.

## CHAPTER XII.

### LIBERAL TREATMENT OF PRISONERS.

Lack of precaution on the part of the English Leaders, 119—Capture of fugitives at the crags near Stirling, 120—Probable number of English slain, 121—Death of Sir Robert Clifford, 122—Sir Marmaduke Twenge becomes prisoner to Bruce, 123—Mowbray surrenders Stirling Castle, 124—The Dead buried in the Field, 125—Edward Bruce captures the Earl of Hereford, 126—The latter is exchanged for several Scottish prisoners, 127.

CONTENTS.

## CHAPTER XIII.

### BENEFICIAL RESULTS OF THE BATTLE.

Robert Baston, the verse-maker, retained, 128—Stores of every kind acquired by the Scots, 129—Bruce distributes the spoil most equitably, 130—Two Knights of Brabant build an Inn at Antwerp, *ib*—Fortifications of Stirling Castle demolished, 131—Rich stuffs preserved in the churches of Scotland, *ib*—Success of Scotland attributed to the interposition of Heaven, 132—Benefit resulting to Scotland from the victory, 133—Her Heroes ought ever to be remembered, 134

## ADDENDA

Great loss of human life in ancient times, 136—Lamentable position of the Scots had they been conquered, 137—Their heroism exhibits a brilliant lesson to the World, *ib*—Who would be free must be true and just men, 139—Essentials whereby a nation can enjoy the blessing of Freedom, *ib*.

|   | PAGE |
|---|---|
| APPENDIX OF NOTES . . | 141 |

## BIOGRAPHICAL NOTICES.

### SCOTTISH WARRIORS.

| | |
|---|---|
| Robert the First . . . . . | 153 |
| Sir Edward Bruce . | 159 |
| Thomas Randolph, Earl of Moray . . . | 161 |
| Sir James Douglas . . . | 164 |
| Walter, the High Steward of Scotland . . | 168 |

### ENGLISH WARRIORS.

| | |
|---|---|
| King Edward the Second . . . . . . | 170 |
| Gilbert de Clare, Earl of Gloucester . | 172 |
| Sir Giles de Argentine . . . . . | 174 |
| Robert Clifford . . . . | 176 |
| Aymer de Valence, Earl of Pembroke . . | 178 |
| Ingram de Umfreville . . . . . | 182 |

# LIST OF ILLUSTRATIONS.

|  | PAGE |
|---|---|
| Map of the Battle-field | 1 |
| Arms of Brus of Annandale | 153 |
| Royal Arms of Scotland | ib. |
| Arms of the Earls of Carrick | 159 |
| Arms of the Earl of Moray | 161 |
| Arms of Sir James Douglas | 164 |
| Arms of Walter, the High Steward | 168 |
| Arms of King Edward the Second | 170 |
| Arms of the Earl of Gloucester | 172 |
| Arms of Sir Giles de Argentine | 174 |
| Arms of Robert Clifford | 176 |
| Arms of the Earl of Pembroke | 178 |
| Arms of De Umfreville | 182 |

# LIST OF AUTHORITIES QUOTED.

*Where size is not indicated, the books are 8vo. Some are 12mo or less.*

ABERCROMBY (P.) Martial Achievements of the Scots Nation. Edinburgh, 1711. 2 vols. fol.

BANKS (T. C.) Baronia Anglica Concentrata. Ripon. 2 vols. 4to.

Barbour (J.) The Life and Acts of the most victorious Conqueror Robert Bruce, King of Scotland. B.L. Edinburgh, 1758. Sm. 4to.

Barbour (J.) The Bruce, published from a MS. dated 1489, with Notes, etc., by John Jamieson, D.D. Edinburgh, 1820. 4to.

Bellenden (J.) History and Chronicles of Scotland, written in Latin by Hector Boece. Translated. Edinburgh, 1821. 2 vols. 4to.

Buchanan (G.) History of Scotland. Translated by James Aikman. London, 1867. 4 vols.

Buckle (H. T.) History of Civilization in England. London, 1867. 3 vols.

Burton (J. H.) History of Scotland. Edinburgh, 1867-70. 7 vols.

CAPGRAVE (J.) The Chronicle of England. Chronicles of Great Britain. London, 1858.

Carte (T.) General History of England. London, 1747-55. 4 vols. fol.

Chalmers (G.) Caledonia; or an Account, Historical and Topographical, of North Britain. London, 1807-24. 3 vols. 4to.

Chaucer (G.) The Works of. B.L. London, 1598. Fol.

Chron. de Lan. Chronicon de Lanercost. Edited by Joseph Stevenson, Esq. Bannatyne Club. Edinburgh, 1839. 4to.

Creasy (E. S.) The Fifteen Decisive Battles of the World. London, 1851. 2 vols.

DUGDALE (W.) The Baronage of England. London, 1675-6. 2 vols. fol.

FŒDERA, Conventiones, Literae, etc., by Thomas Rymer and Robert Sanderson. London, 1704-35. 20 vols. fol.

xxii  AUTHORITIES.

Fordun (J. de) Scotichronicon, cum Supplementis, etc  Edinburgh, 1759.  2 vols. fol.

GODSCROFT.  The History of the Houses of Douglas and Angus, by David Hume of Godscroft.  Edinburgh, 1644  Sm fol
Gordon (P )  The Famous History of the Renown'd and Valiant Prince Robert, sirnamed the Bruce, etc.  Edinburgh, 1718.
Grey (T.)  Scalacronica, Edited by Joseph Stevenson, Esq., Maitland Club.  Edinburgh, 1836.  4to
Grote (G )  History of Greece.  London, 1862  8 vols
Guillim (J.)  Display of Heraldry.  London, 1724.  Fol

HAILES' Annals of Scotland, by Sir D. Dalrymple, Lord Hailes.  Edinburgh, 1779  2 vols. 4to.
Hall (E )  The Union of the Two Noble Houses of Lancaster and York.  𝔅.𝔏.  London, 1550  4to.
Hardyng (J.)  The Chronicle of, with continuation by Richard Grafton.  London, 1812.  4to.
Henry (R )  The History of Great Britain  London, 1805  12 vols.
Herodotus, The History of, Translated by George Rawlinson.  London, 1858.  4 vols
Hollinshed (R )  The Historie of Scotland  𝔅.𝔏.  London, 1586.  Fol
Hume (D.)  The History of England  London, 1808  10 vols.

INNES (C.)  Scotland in the Middle Ages.  Edinburgh, 1860.

KERR (R.)  History of Scotland during the reign of Robert the First, sirnamed The Bruce.  Edinburgh, 1811.  2 vols

LELAND (J.)  De Rebus Britannicis Collectanea.  Hearne, London, 1770  6 vols
Leland (J.)  The Itinerary.  Hearne, Oxford, 1770.  9 vols.
Lingard (J.)  The History of England  London, 1849.  10 vols.
Lockhart.  The Lockhart Papers  London, 1817.  2 vols. 4to.

MACAULAY (T B )  The History of England  London, 1849-61  5 vols
Meyrick (S R )  A Critical Inquiry into Ancient Armour.  London, 1824  3 vols fol.
Middleton (T.)  Dramatic Works.  London, 1840  5 vols.
Mon Malms.  Monachi cujusdam Malmsburiensis vita Edwardi Secundi.  Oxon, 1729.
Moore (Thos de la )  Vita et Mors Edwardi II.  Camdeni Anglica Normanica, etc.  Francofurti, 1603.

## AUTHORITIES.

Nimmo (W.)  History of Stirlingshire.  Stirling, 1817.  2 vols.

Nisbet (A.)  A System of Heraldry.  Edinburgh, 1816.  2 vols. fol.

North<sup>d</sup>. Book.  The Household Book of Henry Algernon Percy, Fifth Earl of Northumberland.  London, 1827.

Raine (J.)  The History and Antiquities of North Durham.  London, 1852.  Fol.

Ridpath (G.)  The Border History of England and Scotland.  London, 1776.  4to.

Rot. Scot.  Rotuli Scotiae, or the Scots Rolls (Public Records).  London, 1824.  2 vols. fol.

Scots Acts.  The Lawes and Actes of the Parliament of Scotland.  Edinburgh, 1597.  Sm. fol.

Scott (W.)  Poetical Works of.  Edinburgh, 1833.  12 vols.

Serres (J. de.)  The Generall Historie of France.  London, 1624.  Fol.

Speed (J.)  The Historie of Great Britaine.  London, 1632.  Fol.

Stewart (W.)  The Buik of the Croniclis of Scotland, or a version of the History of Hector Boece.  (Chronicles of Great Britain.)  London, 1858.  3 vols.

Stow (J.)  Annales, or a General Chronicle of England.  London, 1631.  Fol.

Taylor (J.)  Pictorial History of Scotland.  London, 1859.  2 vols.

Thucydides, History of, translated by S. T. Bloomfield.  London, 1829.  3 vols.

Turner (S.)  The History of England during the Middle Ages.  London, 1825.  5 vols.

Tyrrel (J.)  The General History of England.  London, 1704.  3 vols. fol.

Tytler (P. F.)  The History of Scotland.  Edinburgh, 1841.  10 vols.

Walsingham (T.)  Quondam Monachi S. Albani Historia Anglicana.  (Chronicles of Great Britain.)  London, 1863.  2 vols.

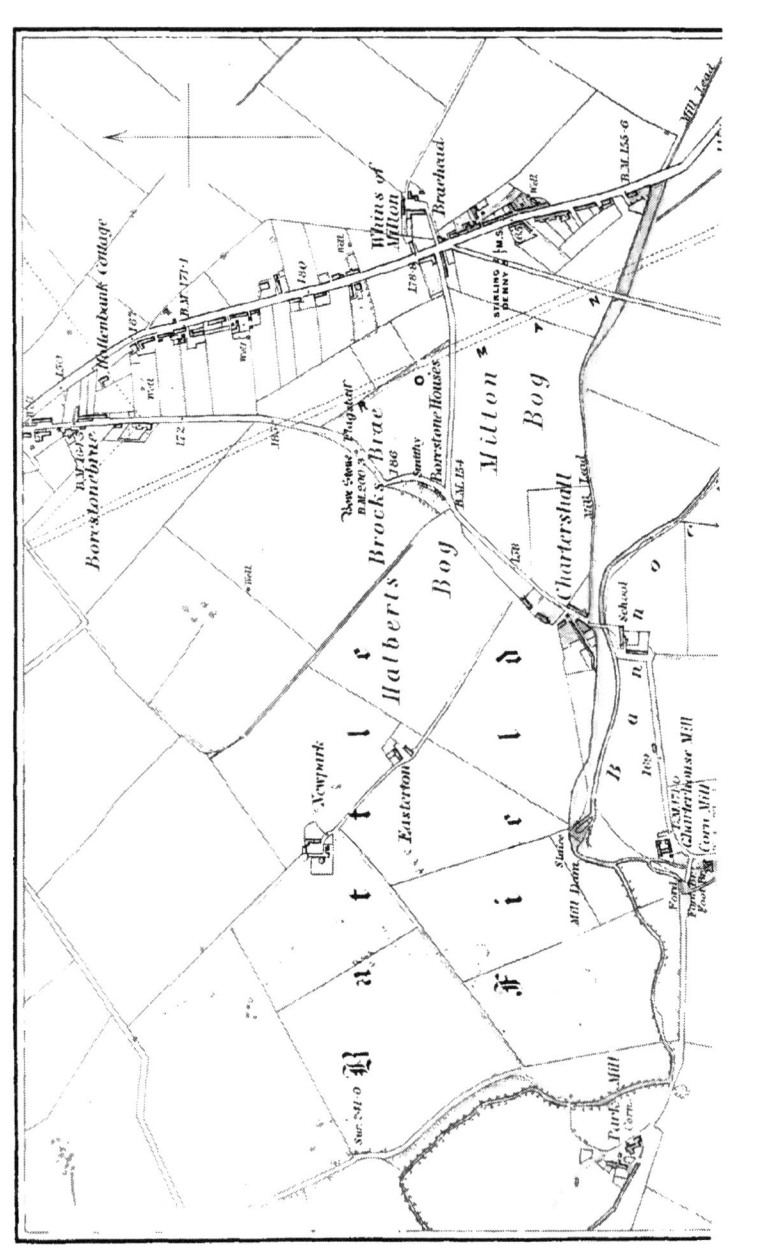

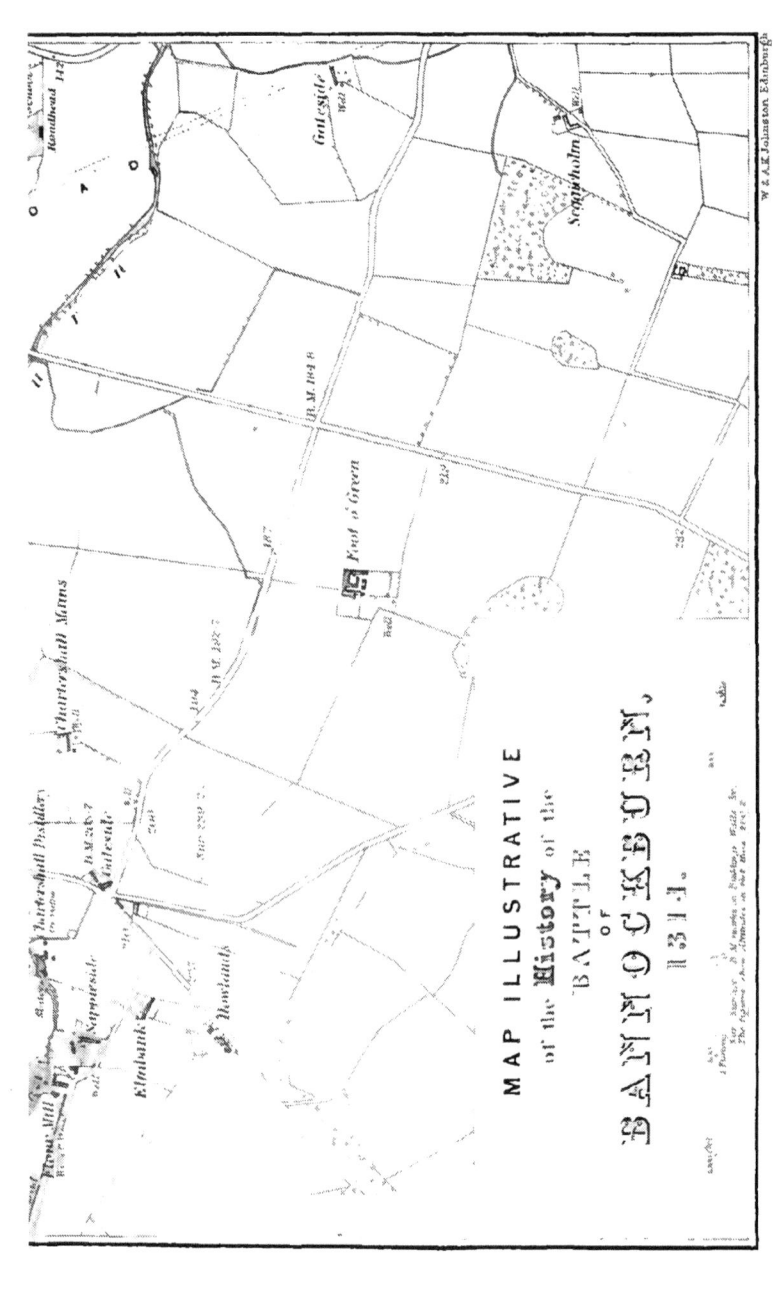

## CHAPTER I.

#### PRELIMINARY OBSERVATIONS.

This land was never formed to harbour slaves;
The rivers syllable we must be free;
The brooks, the burns, re-echo forth the tale;
The very winds that sweep the rugged hills,
The hurricanes that shake the mountain tops,
All, all resound with liberty to man!

ANON.

IN 1285, on the death of Alexander the Third, and even down to the decease of his grand-daughter, Margaret of Norway, in 1290, the people of Scotland were in the enjoyment of much comfort and prosperity. After that period, however, by the aggressive movements of Edward the First of England, they were subjected to a course of trial and suffering of the most severe kind, which lasted almost a quarter of a century. Her nobles and principal men unfortunately were more ready to promote their own personal interest than advance the independence of their country, hence they separated from each other, and the cause of patriotism suffered accordingly. Many arranged themselves on the side of England, while only a few proved true men, resolving to maintain the glory and honour of Scotland. The middle classes and peasantry, ever subject to oppression from those above them, were levied time after time to form the ranks of defensive war, and when we consider the numerous conflicts in which they were engaged, and the exterminating tendency of these broils, it appears strange that such numbers still survived, on whose strength both Wallace and Bruce were able to contend with, and often to overcome, their more powerful enemies.[1] The lands also, which in the time of David the First, from proper cultivation, produced excellent crops, were now neglected, and had it not been that sheep and cattle were still kept in those districts seldom visited by the English, that deer and other game were found in the wild uplands, and fish in the rivers and sea, many poor people must have died of hunger.[2]

About the period from 1290 to 1314 Scotland presented a very different aspect from what we behold at present. Nearly all its valleys, and large portions of its low-lying ground, were densely covered with trees and brushwood, which had grown up without any aid from the

---

[1] Among the marvels of former times, that of the resistance shown by the inhabitants of Caledonia to the Roman armies stands prominently forward. Innumerable legions of martial men, who, by their love of battle, their armour and discipline, overcame every other country they assailed, found their valour of slight avail here. Our uncivilised ancestors, living in woods, huts, or caves, unknowing in the arts, and almost without the means of forging an implement of war, so effectually beat back the conquerors of the world, that the latter had to erect a huge wall, nearly seventy miles long, to protect themselves from the assaults of these terrible northern warriors. That barrier is another wonder to all intellectual men, and its very remains constitute the highest compliment ever paid to the people of any land, for their bravery, their love of liberty, and their determination, at whatever cost, to live or die free men.

[2] 'The contest that ensued was of unexampled length and severity, and, in its sad course, the Scotch, notwithstanding their heroic resistance, and the victories they occasionally gained, had to endure every evil which could be inflicted by their proud and insolent neighbour.'—*Buckle*, vol. iii. p. 13

hand of man.[3] These forests, in many places, where the land consisted of mountain and dale, ascended far up the sides of the hills, affording shelter and sustenance to those wild beasts of chase which were common to the country.[4] The higher and more open ranges were often wild and barren, which, under attention, might have afforded food for sheep or cattle; but where these did not exist, the wide moors became waste land, dry and unproductive in summer, while throughout winter they were soaked in water. Interspersed here and there were extensive morasses tufted with heather, but below, soft moss many feet deep formed swamps altogether impassable to man or beast. Green spots might be seen around villages, and at no great distance from towns, which had once been under the plough; but Nature was again resuming her sway, silently but surely, over the efforts of man, while many a fair field and broad acre, which we see pastured by thriving sheep and cattle, or waving with ripening grain in harvest, were covered then with gorse, bent, and heath, awaiting more peaceable times, that they might be turned to good account for the benefit and improvement of society.

In the brilliant pages of Macaulay[5] we have a striking picture of the badness of the highways in England during the reign of Charles the Second, but in Scotland, at the commencement of the fourteenth century, very few roads intersected the country, and these, from their imperfect state, could hardly be accounted public ways, save one or two

---

[3] 'There is every sort of proof that every district of Caledonia, as the name implies, was anciently covered with woods.'—*Chalmers*, vol. i. p. 791.

[4] 'The face of the country was covered by immense forests, chiefly of oak.'—*Tytler*, vol. ii. p. 166.   [5] Vol. i. pp. 371-4.

direct lines of transit which had been formed eleven hundred years before by the Romans. When the soil over which any of these had been made was soft or liable to be washed away by rain, they were only tracks whereon a man might travel on horseback, but altogether unfit for carriages save in the time of summer. Others of less length might be found between inland towns, and, occasionally, from these to places on the seashore, for the purposes of import or export, and such lines had been constructed principally by the order of monks of several establishments, who, to their credit be it said, in early times were ever ready to promote the welfare of the people. The lands and houses they possessed were let to tenants—a part of the rent only to be paid in money, and the rest in manual service; and these landlords clearly perceived the advantage of having access to the nearest ports, whereby they might sell what produce they could spare, and purchase other commodities of which they were in want. The towns were small, few, and thinly populated, the inhabitants being chiefly dealers in small wares, weavers, shoemakers, joiners, and smiths, although the scope of the latter trades was very limited, because, from a very early date down to the beginning of the fifteenth century, not only rustic implements employed in agriculture, but armour, spears, bows, and arrows, were imported from Flanders.[6]

---

[6] *Buckle*, vol iii. pp. 23-4.—In 1425 'it is ordaned be the King and the Parliament, that all merchands of the realm, passand over sea for merchandice, bring hame, as he maie gudly thoile, after the quantity of his merchandice, harnes and armoures, with speares, schaftes, bowes, and staues. And that be done be ilk ane of them als oft as it happenis them to passe ouer sea in merchandice.'—*Scots Acts*, fol 7.

Throughout the period of which we intend to treat, cultivation of the ground was overlooked, corn crops were neither sown nor reaped,[7] all other domestic pursuits were neglected, while the strength and genius of the male population were by circumstances directed to one object only, and that was war.

We may therefore perceive that much attention was paid to the equipment of men for the field, and by the intercourse Scotland maintained with the Continent, Robert Bruce and his knights were arrayed after the most approved fashion.[8] By that monarch's seal, he appears mounted on horseback, his arms and legs are covered with linked mail, the spur of the nearest being plainly visible. His helmet is cylindrical, with openings something like the letter T, and pierced also with square holes, while the top is adorned with a crown, on which are three ornamental crosses, or *fleurs-de-lis*, between each of which is a point, or precious stone. His body-armour, which consisted probably of steel plate, is covered by the surcoat, on which is shown the Scottish lion, and the same noble animal is depicted on the housings both on the shoulder and the hind-quarter of his horse. The like emblem figures within the double tressure on his shield, which is borne on his left arm, and the ends of the cross-bar of his sword are turned slightly upwards from the right hand

---

[7] 'The labourers either fled or were murdered, and there being no one to till the ground, some of the fairest parts of Scotland were turned into a wilderness, overgrown with briars and thickets.' —*Buckle*, vol. iii. pp. 16-7.

[8] 'The knight and noble, before the days of Robert Bruce, rode armed in mail, always of foreign manufacture, from Flanders or Italy.'—*Innes*, pp. 128-9.

which grasps it. His brother, Sir Edward Bruce, his nephew, Thomas Randolph Earl of Moray, young Walter the High Steward, and James Douglas, all wore defensive armour, including shields, after the same manner. The knights and horse-soldiers were similarly equipped, and the offensive weapons of the whole were each a long lance,[9] a battle-axe slung from the shoulder, a sword on the left, and a long knife or dagger on the right side. The armour of the foot-soldiers were each a skull-cap of iron, first brought into use by their countryman Michael Scott, of wizard fame,[10] a hanketon or garment of leather,[11] on which folds of cloth were quilted, reaching from the neck to below the knee, and covering the arms so as to ward off either thrust or blow. They were armed nearly in the same way as the horsemen, having each a target or shield made of light but tough material, such as skin, a pike or spear[12] eighteen feet in length, a battle-axe, also a sword

---

[9] 'Lance was the word used at the time for the peculiar weapon of the cavalry.'—*Meyrick*, vol. i p. 187.

[10] 'At this time (*circa* 1245) flourished Michael Scott, the domestic astrologer of the Emperor Frederic II., who invented the use of that armour for the head which is called cervelliere.'—*Meyrick*, vol. i. p. 141.

[11] 'They are onelie couered with leather pilches made of bucks' skins.'—*Hollinshed*, p. 218.

[12] 'The Scotch spear was six elns long, or five elns 'before the burr,' ' of a clyft,' that is of one piece, a length which, at least in later times, obliged the spear-staves to be drawn from foreign countries. A fully-armed Scotch soldier had one of these formidable pikes, an axe, with a knife for finishing the work which these might leave imperfect, and a large shield of hide, 'to resist the shot of England.'—*Notes to 'The Brus,' by Innes*, p. 518. The burr was a broad iron ring fixed on the tilting lance behind the handle. It is shown in a cut in *Guillim*, p. 340. See also Hall's *Henry IV*, fol xii, and *Middleton*, vol. ii p 465

and a strong knife for use in close combat. The archers were not so well defended as the spearmen, for they were without shields, but in addition to the bow and ample sheaf of arrows, they had the sword, the dagger, and battle-axe, which was used with deadly effect upon knights and men-at-arms when thrown to the ground. Scotland had few mounted warriors, and these rode small horses, consequently her defenders were unable to cope with the chivalry of England, troops of whom were covered, horse and man, in complete mail. Each Scottish knight was attended by two, three, or more squires, who waited upon him, held his horse, enabled him to mount, and bore such portions of his equipment as he might require in battle.[13] The man-at-arms likewise had his sergeants to perform the same round of duties. Accordingly, a regular army of foot and horse in England or Scotland, whether stationary or on the march, was always accompanied by a promiscuous multitude of male and female followers, amounting in number to two-thirds or more of the martial men, and these gave assistance to the regular soldiers in seeking water, preparing food, washing, repairing clothes and harness, and cleaning weapons and armour of every description.[14]

Before this period the arrangement of an army in battle-array was most simple. In the early ages, and

---

[13] 'And every knight had after him riding
Three henshmen on him awaiting.'
*Chaucer*, f. 367.

[14] The same order prevailed in ancient times, for when the army of Xerxes was brought from Asia into Greece, we have the authority of Herodotus in saying that the number of 'camp-followers' considerably exceeded that of the fighting men.

down to the fifteenth century, to lead the right wing was always considered as the chief post of honour.[15] This arose from the front lines bearing the shield on the left arm, consequently that side was best defended, and the assailing troops had thereby the least chance of vanquishing their opponents.[16] But towards the fourteenth century the preparation for battle, both in England and Scotland, exhibited no great amount of either skill or genius.[17] The infantry on either side was usually placed in several bodies, each under its respective leader, and between these, or near the wings, were the companies of archers, often divided, but when the ground was favourable keeping together, that their shafts might tell with more deadly effect on any particular quarter of the enemy. Much importance, however, was now placed on the English cavalry, who frequently succeeded in breaking through the opposing lines of the foe, and this usually was the first step towards victory. Sometimes, if an overpowering stroke was intended, they made the first charge on the Scots at full gallop; but again, they often remained either behind the divisions of infantry, or near the flanks of the army,

---

[15] 'The right wing was the special point of honour.'—*Herodotus*, vol. iii. p. 500, note.

[16] 'Engaging hand to hand, the shield, the principal defence, being borne on the left arm, was less a protection for the right side; and the soldier in the extreme of the right wing, to avoid exposing the undefended part of his body, would always rather incline to the right. The man, then, next to the left, and so every man in the line, would also press toward the right, to profit from the protection of his neighbour's shield.'—*Note by Mitford in Thucydides*, vol. ii. p. 524.

[17] 'There was nothing peculiar to Scotland in tactics before the days of Robert Bruce.'—*Innes*, p. 128.

ready to enter whenever an opening was made in the opposite columns. Robert Bruce knew all this, and, with that penetrative wisdom for which he was so remarkable, began at once to introduce regular order among his men, enforcing them not to break the line of battle. It was in strict observance of this design that he was in a great measure indebted to his good fortune at Bannockburn. General order was subsequently observed on commencing battle, both by the English and Scots, but in the heat of conflict it was occasionally neglected, for often 'groom fought like noble, squire like knight,' and every true man, from the King to the meanest soldier, performed his part therein to the best of his power. At Agincourt, Henry the Fifth was not only beaten down on his knees, but was 'repeatedly struck upon his helmet and armour,' and when 'his brother, the Duke of Gloucester, was felled senseless at his feet, the King immediately stood over him, repelled a long and furious attack to take him, and had the gratification to preserve his life.'[18]

In England, among the various classes of combatants, the knights and men-at-arms, from the weight and force of their charge, as has been observed, were considered almost invincible. Through every nation in Europe, such warriors were renowned, for they usually came off victorious in battle; till in 1302, on the 11th July, near Courtray in Belgium, the brave Flemings, under John of Namur, encountered on foot the mailed chivalry of France, and won the victory, after which 4000 gilt spurs were found on the field.[19] Tidings of this change in the mode of warfare circulated all over the known world, so that Bruce

---

[18] *Turner*, vol. ii. p. 435.     [19] *Serres*, p. 152.

drew conclusions from it, which were of essential service to himself through all his future career. In 1307, between two morasses east of Loudon Hill, his lines of serried spearmen repulsed the attack of a gallant body of English cavalry led by De Valence, Earl of Pembroke, and put them to flight.[20] He had also the sagacity to perceive that Wallace was vanquished at the battle of Falkirk, after his cavalry had shamefully fled, by the English knights and men-at-arms surrounding his bodies or schiltrums[21] of spearmen, and steadily destroying them after all chance of retreat for the unfortunate men was cut off. Weighing every circumstance, he thereby perceived his main chance of success lay in selecting a suitable piece of ground for battle whereon to place his army, so that they could not possibly be outflanked, but have sufficient room whereon to meet the enemy in deadly encounter. Valiant and powerful though Bruce was at any moment in the use of his weapons, he was at the same time wise, considerate, and cautious, never failing in judgment when an important case came before him, but, according to circumstances, ever deciding for the best.

---

[20] The lowest morass, that to the south-east of the spot, is now drained and bearing crops. Kerr, in his *History of Scotland*, says, 'The spearmen were probably drawn up in a solid phalanx or deep battalion, and if arrayed in eight ranks, which long afterwards continued to be the order of such troops, six hundred men would present a front of seventy-five files, covering a space of about fifty yards, allowing two feet for each man.'—Vol i. p. 308.

[21] *Schiltrum*, a mass of men, large or small, crowded together in a square or circular form

## CHAPTER II.

#### MUSTERING OF FORCES.

> The names of Wallace and Bruce exert a magic influence in this country. They are the demi-gods of our heroic ages; their memory recalls to us the pride of independent Scotland.
> SCOTT.

AFTER Edward the Second, in 1307, ascended the throne of England, instead of directing his attention to the well-being of his kingdom, he continued, as he had done in the lifetime of his father, to prefer the company of favourites to that of his nobility, and bestowed upon the former royal grants and rewards,[1] whereby he incurred the displeasure and hostility of the latter. Differences accordingly arose between them, each carrying out their own measures; and during this period, when the English monarch partly relaxed his hold of the reins by which he held Scotland in subjection, Robert Bruce availed himself of the opportunity, and, by aid from his faithful adherents, strove to liberate that land from the thraldom[2] which the first Edward had

---

[1] A list of rare articles, chiefly of gold and silver, which were in possession of Piers Gaveston, occupies five pages, 388-392, of the *Fœdera*, vol. iii.

[2] 'Thus gat levyt thai, and in sic thrillage;
Bath pur, and thai off hey perage.
For off the lordis sum thai slew;
And sum thai hangyt, and sum thai drew;
And sum thai put in presoune,
For owtyn causs, or enchesoun.'—*Barbour*, p. 11.

imposed upon it. He himself, from the time he was crowned at Scone in 1306, had undergone great privation both of body and mind; but a better prospect now opened up before him, and he took advantage of the occurrence, nobly turning it to the best account.

In 1310, the estates of Scotland,[3] actuated by Bruce, having met at Dundee, solemnly declared that Robert, Lord of Annandale, the competitor, ought by the laws of Scotland to have been preferred to Baliol in competition for the crown; and they recognised Robert Bruce, his grandson, now reigning, as their just and lawful king, engaging to defend his right and the independence of Scotland against all opponents of every rank or dignity; and declaring that whoever contravened the same should be guilty of treason, and held as traitors to the nation.[4]

A pastoral declaration was also issued by the representatives of the church, with the bishops and others, 'that the Scots nation, seeing the kingdom betrayed and enslaved, had assumed Robert Bruce for their king, and that the clergy had willingly done homage to him in that character.' This, it would appear, was only a repetition of a manifesto issued previously by twelve bishops of Scotland, to which their names were all attached, and it ran nearly in the same words. By this means Bruce showed the greatest wisdom. He thereby disarmed the papal thunder of all its power, both in favouring England, and in endeavouring to crush himself and his fellow-patriots by excommunication. These measures were of immense

---

[3] *The Three Estates* of Parliament; the lords, including the prelates, the barons, and the burgesses

[4] Instrument in the General Register House, Edinburgh, alluded to by *Kerr*, vol 1 pp. 370-1.

consequence to him in the promotion of his design, and they had their full effect among a people who regarded the church with the utmost deference and respect.[5]

About this time, or previously, according to Buchanan,[6] Sir John de Menteith, who basely betrayed Wallace, still held possession of the castle of Dumbarton for the King of England. Robert Bruce was induced to enter into negotiation with him for its surrender, and Menteith demanded in return the earldom of Lennox. That honour was held by one of the King's steady supporters, who, when he came to know the proposed terms, generously insisted that his sovereign should complete the exchange. The agreement at length being solemnly ratified, Bruce went to receive possession of the place, and in passing the wood of Colquhoun near Dumbarton, Rolland, a carpenter, sought an interview with him, and told him that a number of armed English were concealed in a cellar of the fortress, so that when the King sat down to dine, these were to come forth and either kill or make him prisoner. Accordingly, when Bruce had obtained the castle, and was looking through the several apartments therein, Menteith asked him to partake of an entertainment, which the King refused till the concealed cellar should be examined. This Menteith attempted to evade by saying that a menial had the key, and would be there presently. Eventually, on breaking up the door, the treachery was revealed, and it was ascertained, that had the plan been successful, a ship was stationed in the firth ready to convey Bruce to England. The traitor was imprisoned, and had suffered death, which he well deserved, but having several beautiful

---

[5] *Kerr*, vol. i. pp. 371-2.     [6] Vol. i. pp. 427-8.

daughters married to wavering but powerful noblemen in the neighbourhood, he was on their account spared. The result will be noticed hereafter. From the note quoted below,[7] we vouch not for the truth of the statement, but it deserves a place, connected as it is with the prowess and good fortune of the Scottish King.

From the trials to which the common people of Scotland were subjected, they became sensible of the inestimable value of freedom, and nobly supported their King in his attempts to rescue the country from bondage. In 1311, a small farmer named William Binnock, at or near Linlithgow, in company with a few armed friends, succeeded in wresting from the English the castle of that ancient town.[8] Robert Bruce, in 1312, recovered from the enemy the castles of Dumfries, Dalswinton, Ayr, and Lanark,[9] besides many other strongholds, the defenders of which, when his force was brought against them, found it desirable to submit to his power. A few months later he laid siege to Perth, and investing it for a time, he took the place near midnight, early in January 1313,[10] himself crossing the ditch which surrounded it, while the water rose to his throat.[11] Very soon afterwards, James Douglas,

---

[7] 'Edward II., inclining to pacific measures, authorised, 2d and 21st August 1309, Richard de Bury, Earl of Ulster, to treat with Bruce; who appointed Sir John de Menteith and Sir Nigel Campbell to conduct this treaty.'—*Fœdera*, vol. iii. pp. 150-163, quoted by *Hailes*, ii. p. 29.

[8] *Hailes*, vol. ii. pp. 32-3.   [9] *Bellenden*, vol. ii. p. 386.

[10] *Chron. de Lan.*, note, p. 415.

[11] ' That tyme wes in his cumpany
A knycht off France, wycht and hardy;
And quhen he in the watyr swa
Saw the king pass, and with him ta

lord of the valley of that name, by the assistance of his trusty followers, won from the enemy the strong fortress of Roxburgh on the eve of Lent, when the garrison therein were enjoying themselves in revelry. This occurred early in March, and on the week following,[12] Thomas Randolph Earl of Moray, after closely investing the castle of Edinburgh, took it also during the night, by escalade, and as the design of Bruce was to demolish all places of defence which the English might possibly occupy, the walls of this and the other fortifications were speedily thrown down.

The castle of Bothwell still remained in possession of England, and this also might possibly have been taken, but another matter of greater importance was at hand. It would appear that Sir Edward Bruce, while his fellows in arms were accomplishing so much, had not been idle, for he captured the castles of Rutherglen and Dundee,[13] and afterwards, in the spring of 1313, laid siege to the castle of Stirling. But the position of this fortress, for it was placed on the summit of a rock, and its natural defences on every side save one, rendered it almost impregnable. The brother of the King, however, continued

---

Hys leddyr wnabasytly,
He saynyt him for the ferly,
And said ; ' A Lord ! quhat sall we say
' Off our lordis off Fraunce, that thai
' With gud morsellis fayreis thair pawnchis,
' And will bot ete, and drynk, and dawnsis ;
' Quhen sic a knycht, and sa worthy
' As this, throw his chewalry,
' Into sic perill has him set,
' To wyn a wrechyt hamillet ? "
*Barbour*, pp. 177-8.

[12] *Hailes*, vol. ii. pp. 37-8.  [13] *Hailes*, vol. ii. p. 40.

to invest it till the middle of summer without any appearance of success, when Sir Philip Mowbray, the governor, a Scotsman in the service of England, arranged with him that if the fortress was not relieved till the nativity of Saint John the Baptist, 24th June of the following year, he would forthwith surrender it to the King of Scotland. Sir Edward was remarkably brave, and a most resolute man, but he lacked the foresight and wisdom of his brother, who in the meantime had invaded Cumberland and conquered the Isle of Man.[14] When the compact was reported to Bruce on his return home,[15] he was very angry, because he at once perceived its impropriety. 'You have done wrong,' said he to his brother, 'and we shall all feel its evil effects, for by such an agreement you allow our powerful enemy a whole year to collect under arms the military force of all his provinces, while we of Scotland will have great difficulty to meet him in the field. Had you pressed Mowbray closely, and not assented to any such stipulation, Stirling Castle in all probability had been ours ere the present year expires.'[16] 'I may have com-

---

[14] *Hailes*, vol. ii. p. 39.   [15] *Bellenden*, vol. ii. pp. 386-7.
[16] ' The King said, quhen he hard the day ;
  ' That wes unwisly doyn perfay !
  ' Ik herd neuir quhar sa lang warnyng
  ' Was gevyn to sa mychty a king,
  ' As is the king off Ingland.
  ' For he has now in till hand
  ' Ingland, Ireland, and Walis alsua,
  ' And Aquitayngné yeit, with all tha ;
  ' And off Scotland yeit a party
  ' Duellis wndre his senyowry.
  ' And off tresour sua stuffyt is he,
  ' That he may wageouris haiff plenté.
  ' And we ar quhoyne agayne sa fele.' '—*Barbour*, p. 216.

mitted an error,' replied Sir Edward, 'but I did it for the best, and if all the warriors he of England can raise will come forward, we will undoubtedly give them battle.'[17] 'Be it so, then,' observed the King, 'we must abide by what you have done. Honour is more dear than life to a true man, and we must do our utmost to confront the strength of England, come when it may.'

Sir Philip Mowbray, having been supplied with a safe-conduct for his journey to and from England, went to London and laid the whole affair before King Edward. Perceiving he was about to lose all ascendency in Scotland, that monarch, on due consideration, resolved to make a desperate effort to retain what had cost his father so much anxiety, and England an enormous amount of human life and treasure. He accordingly entered upon the necessary preparations for the accomplishment of his design, and that his force might be augmented to the greatest possible number, he pardoned all who were implicated in the death of Gaveston.[18] This was so acceptable to the English people, that the earls, barons, knights, and community granted the king, to enable him to carry on the war in Scotland, a *twentieth*, while the citizens and burgesses supplied him with a *fifteenth* of their goods.[19] He likewise endeavoured to borrow money from the clergy to defray the cost of the expedition. Directing his atten-

---

[17] ' Schir Eduuard said, ' Sa God me rede !
   ' Thocht he, and all that he may led,
   ' Cum ; we sall fecht all, war thai ma.''
*Barbour*, p. 216.

[18] The document is dated at Westminster, 16th October 1313. The names occupy nearly four pages in the *Fœdera*, vol. iii. pp. 443-6.

[19] *Carte*, vol. ii. p. 332.

tion to the Continent, he sent for the bravest of his vassals from Gascony, and enlisted troops from Flanders and other foreign states which were in any way under his influence.[20] In England he summoned all the great vassals of the crown, consisting of ninety-three barons, to bring with them the whole feudal force of the kingdom in arms, with horse and accompaniments, and meet him at Berwick, on Monday, the 10th June of the following year.[21] Similar commands were also sent to the leaders of his English subjects in Ireland; and letters were directed to Eth O'Connor, Prince of Connaught, and twenty-five Irish chiefs, that they should muster their followers under Richard de Burgh, Earl of Ulster, and come over to assist him against Robert Bruce.[22] Two days afterwards he appointed Aymer de Valence, Earl of Pembroke, to be Governor of Scotland, and sent him thither to be ready on the royal arrival. Commands were also issued to the Mayors of the several seaport towns of England and Wales, that they should not only send forth the ships they had ready, but equip an additional fleet to assist in the war against the Scots. When the king, on his progress northward,[23]

---

[20] *Hume*, vol. iii. p. 17. Our latest historians, Hailes, Tytler, and Taylor, take no notice of these foreign auxiliaries, but Barbour is sufficient authority. During his journeys into France he would learn much respecting the second Edward.

[21] Summons dated at Westminster, 23d December 1313. *Fœdera*, vol iii. pp. 463-4.

[22] Dated at Westminster, 22d March 1314. *Fœdera*, vol. iii. pp 476-7.

[23] On Easter day, which fell on the 7th April, the King was at Ely; on the 20th April he was at Lincoln; on the 27th he was at Beverley; and at York from the 6th to the 12th of May. *Rot. Scot.*, vol. 1. pp. 123-6.

arrived at Newminster Abbey, near Morpeth, on the 27th May, he sent to the Sheriffs of York and seventeen other counties of England and Wales, orders to array 21,500 foot soldiers, who were to be at Werk on Tweedside, before the 10th June.[24] These bands of infantry, which the King so earnestly demanded, ought to have been with him some days previously, had his former mandates been observed.[25] Besides all these forces, he had still many adherents in Scotland, who for their own interest performed his commands, and who were prepared to take their place in his ranks when he arrived in that country.[26] Moreover, he

---

[24] It appears he had learned at this point of his journey, how and where Bruce intended to give him battle, as the following translation from the original order in Latin will show :—' The King to the Sheriff of Yorkshire wisheth health. As, for the expedition in our Scots war, we have chosen four thousand men from your county, whom we have ordered to attend us into Scotland on the day already mentioned, and as we now learn that the Scots, our enemies and rebels, are using their utmost efforts to collect a great multitude of infantry, in strong and marshy places, where access is difficult for cavalry; that, placing themselves between us and our castle of Stirling, they may thereby oppose the rescue of our said castle with all their power: which rescue must be made upon the next ensuing festival of the nativity of St. John the Baptist, according to the agreement entered into between the constable of our said castle and our said enemies; and which rescue, with the blessing of divine aid, we propose then to accomplish,' etc.—*Fœdera*, vol. iii. pp. 481-2. 'The orders to the Sheriffs and others having authority in the several counties of England and Wales, were extremely peremptory; and they were commanded to urge, hasten, and compel the several required quotas, under the highest penalties, to march in a state of sufficient preparation, and fitly armed, so as to join the royal army at Werk.'—*Kerr*, vol. i. pp. 434-5.

[25] *Ridpath*, p. 243.

[26] 'Of Scotland he had yet then
A great many of worthy men.'—*Barbour*, B. L. p. 224.

invested John Duke of Argyle with the title of High Admiral of the western fleet of England; and, as that nobleman possessed many ships, he was appointed to co-operate with those of the king, that the whole movement might be perfect for the entire subjugation of the Scots. He had likewise to arrange that provision for the troops and forage for the cavalry should be provided in regular order throughout the course of his expedition. Numbers of masons, carpenters, smiths, and armourers, were also engaged to accompany the fighting men; while waggons, cars, and beasts of burden, were required to convey the pavilions, baggage, and other necessary articles of so large an army.[27]

Robert Bruce and his adherents, heroic men, actuated by noble enthusiasm, did all in their power to increase the army of Scotland. Nearly all the people of the kingdom, save those of the eastern portion of Berwickshire, and on the coast northward beyond Dunbar, had submitted to the sway of Bruce, and, as has been observed, what told effectually toward his success, the clergy, judging truly of the important crisis, were wholly in his favour. Every intellectual Scotsman was aware how his country had been harassed and his fellow-men slaughtered by the English, while the murder of Wallace, the gallant, the patriotic, the devoted defender of all that was sacred in his own land, caused among his countrymen, who were 'trained to arms in stern misfortune's field,' an irrepressible feeling of wrath and resentment.[28] During a continued struggle of eight

---

[27] *Rot. Scot.* vol. 1. pp 113-28.

[28] They were 'hardened with continual use of war, and, by reason that on the points of their swords and spears they carried along with them all their hopes of life, liberty, honour, and wealth,

years, King Robert, by his prudence, prowess, and sagacity, caused them to hope that if they stood truly to him, and gave him all the support they could yield, better days were in prospect than any they had yet seen. When a proclamation, therefore, went forth that the warriors of these districts of Scotland who were favourable to Bruce should come forward ready for battle, it was obeyed with wonderful celerity, and, considering the depressed state of the kingdom, with its lack of the very means of war, it seems astonishing how such numbers of active men could be drawn thence in defence of all that we in more favourable times hold venerable and dear.[29]

Mention has been made of Sir John de Menteith being imprisoned on account of his treachery to Bruce. At this time, as the King had to 'contend for the safety of the State,' lest the noblemen who had married the daughters of the traitor should be incited to revenge, he liberated Menteith—'his sons-in-law being his sureties'—on condi-

---

were unspeakably resolute and fierce. Besides, they had *at* their head a leader who alone was worth multitudes; nothing escaped the depth of his penetration and forecast.'—*Abercromby*, vol. i. p. 595.

[29] 'Speed messengers the country through;
Arouse old friends and gather new;
Warn Lanark's knights to gird their mail,
Rouse the brave sons of Teviotdale,
Let Ettrick's archers sharp their darts,
The fairest forms, the truest hearts!
Call all, call all! from Redeswire path,
To the wild confines of Cape Wrath;
Wide let the news through Scotland ring,
The Northern Eagle claps his wing!'
*Scott*, vol. x. pp. 215 17.

tion that the wavering chieftain should take up his position in front of the first impending battle whenever it might take place.[30]

King Edward would appear to have remained at Newminster Abbey till about the 7th day of June, and then proceeded to Berwick, where he lingered probably to receive the last levies of his great army from England and Ireland. On the 18th June he quitted Berwick with his forces, and held on his way to Edinburgh.[31] When Robert Bruce heard he had crossed the Tweed with such a splendid array of martial men, he made arrangement that his whole power[32] should instantly assemble at the Torwood, a few miles north-west of Falkirk. To this place of meeting Sir Edward Bruce came, and brought with him all the able men he could muster; so also did Walter the Steward and James Douglas, who exerted themselves most manfully in endeavouring to make Scotland free. Nor was Randolph Earl of Moray behind his fellows in the noble enterprise, and the exertions of all to bring so many fighting men together were most gratifying to the gallant Bruce. He himself was accompanied by his devoted

---

[30] *Buchanan*, vol. i. p. 428.   [31] *Henry*, vol. vii. p. 140.
[32] 'His royal summons warn'd the land,
   That all who own'd their king's command
   Should instant take the spear and brand,
      To combat at his side
   O who may tell the sons of fame
   That at King Robert's bidding came,
      To battle for the right!
   From Cheviot to the shores of Ross,
   From Solway Sands to Marshall's-Moss,
      All boun'd them for the fight.'
               *Scott*, vol. x. p. 228.

followers, and he found that the warriors who assembled round him numbered upwards of thirty thousand.[33] Besides these, apart from the immediate attendants on the knights

---

[33] 'The king Robert, quhen he hard say
That Inglis men in sic aray,
And in to sua gret quantité,
Come in his land ; in hy gert he
His men be somound generaly.
And thai come all, full wilfully,
To the Torwod, quhar that the king
Had ordanyt to mak thair meting.
Schir Eduuard the Bruce, the worthi,
Come with a full gret cumpany
Off gud men, armyt weill at rycht,
Hardy, and forsy for to fycht.
Waltre, stewart of Scotland syne,
That than wes bot a berdles hyne,
Come with a rout of noble men,
That men mycht be contynence ken.
The gud lord of Dowglas alsua
Broucht with him men, Ik wndreta
That weile war wsyt in fechting.

\* \* \* \*

The erle off Murreff, with his men
Arayit weile, come alsua then
In to gud cowyne for to fycht,
And gret will for to manteym thair mycht.
Owtakyn, thair mony barownys,
And knychtis that of gret renowne is,
Come with thair men full stalwartly.
Quhen thai war assemblyt halely,
Off fechtand men I trow thai war
Thretty thowsand, and sum dele mar ;
For owtyn cariage and pettaill,
That yemyt harnayis and wictaill.'

*Barbour,* pp. 221-2.

and cavalry, were the camp-followers of every description, who might amount to above fifteen thousand men. Here, on the openings among the trees, they had ample room for movement, for tradition says that Torwood once extended from the banks of the Carron, in the parish of Dunipace, far into that of St. Ninian's, at Tor-brex, near Stirling. This range of greenwood, in the memory of many of these warriors, afforded shelter repeatedly to Wallace and his gallant followers, when hardly beset by the English under Edward the First.

## CHAPTER III.

### LOCALITIES CONNECTED WITH THE BATTLE.

When Edward came to vanquish Caledon,
How did the Bruce contrive to stay the march
Of England's mighty host?  Was the ground flat,
Or hilly he selected, where his troops
Drove back the fierce invaders and achieved
Glory to Scotland, whereby every son
Born in her bounds was henceforth to be free ?

ANON.

WHEN King Edward proceeded northward from Berwick with the whole martial strength of England, we learn from our most authentic chroniclers that no army of such magnitude had ever before crossed the Borders. Rejecting the account of one or two authors[1] as undeserving of credit on that point, we may fairly estimate the number of the whole effective men to have been above one hundred thousand. Of these forty thousand were cavalry, including knights and men-at-arms, of whom more than a twelfth part had horses clothed in mail, who were intended to form the van in the field of battle.[2] The archers are said to have num-

---

[1] *Major* and *Bellenden*, who were followed partly by *Bower*, the continuator of *Fordun*.

[2] ' Ane hundre thousand men and ma :
And fourty thousand war of tha
Armyt on hors, bath heid and hand.
And off thai yeit war thre thousand,
With helyt horss in plate and mailye,
To mak the front off the batailye.'

*Barbour*, p. 218.

bered about fifty thousand,³ and the remainder consisted of billmen and spearmen, who in combat were to take their places between the divisions of the cavalry. Of the chief leaders expected by the king, four were absent, namely, the Earls of Lancaster, Warenne, Warwick, and Arundel,⁴ who alleged, by way of excuse, he had failed in performing to them certain promises, but they each sent their contingent of horsemen and infantry.⁵ In the order of march they were separated into ten divisions, each numbering about ten thousand armed men.⁶

Much is left for our imagination to fill up when we contemplate the appearance of the great army of England wending its way over hill and dale, through forest and glade, by the banks of the streams and across the broad open wastes of the south of Scotland. A strain of lofty poetry is discernible in the verses of the venerable Archdeacon of Aberdeen, when he describes the pomp and magnificence of the splendid spectacle,⁷ under the rays of a bright summer sun. The chief warriors ap-

---

[3] 'And fyfty thousand off archeris
He had, for owytyn hobeleris
And men of fute [and smal rangale,]
That yemyt harnays and wietaile.'—*Barbour*, p. 218.

[4] *Walsingham*, vol 1 pp 139-40.   [5] *Carte*, vol. ii. p. 333.

[6] 'The king, throu consaile of his men,
His folk delt in bataillis ten.
In ilkane war weile ten thousand,
That lete thai stalwartly suld stand
In the bataile, and stythly fycht,
And leve nocht for thair fayis mycht.'
*Barbour*, pp. 219-20

[7] 'As the batailhs, that wai braid,
Departyt our the feldis raid.

peared in their most sumptuous array, with surcoats embroidered in various bright colours,[8] exhibiting their respective bearings, and covering such plate armour as they then wore, while above them, fluttering in the breeze,

---

> The sone wes brycht, and schynand cler.
> And armouris that burnysyt wer,
> Swa blomyt with the sonnys beme,
> That all the land wes in a leme.
> Baneris rycht fayrly flawmand,
> And penselys to the wynd wawand.'
>
> Barbour, pp. 220-1.

[8] In a translation of a French poem, by William Guiart, the description of a battle, under the year 1304, throws much light on the elaborate equipment of an English knight at that period.

> 'The furniture of stamped gold
> Which they have upon their armour
> With its beautiful interlacings,
> Is of such superior kind as to be astonishing:
> Of Indian silk, white, vermilion,
> Yellow, green, reddish yellow, light and blue,
> Free from spot or blemish:
> And which is not put on in heaps,
> But great care taken of the little lions,
> The little birds, and little beasts,
> Which in neat and polished work,
> Appear there in different colours.
> Such things cannot be called to mind without griefs.
> In short, which is so agreeable,
> Rose, ruddy, argent, and sable,
> Vermilion, azure, and metal,
> Which these fine arrangements set in order,
> Shining forth with attraction,
> In rich shields and saddles,
> In girdles and in tissues,
> On those who issue from the field.'
>
> Meyrick, vol. i. p. 190.

was a forest extending for miles in every direction, of banners and flags, emblazoned in gold and other dazzling hues, and these again were everywhere intermingled still more densely with the long slender pennons and streamers of rich silk waving from the heads of the spears borne by the knights, who always held them aloft on the journey.[9] These were all marshalled in due order, according to the respective ranks of the nobles, and in strict conformity to the regulations of heraldry. A troop of horsemen probably led the way first, then several squadrons of archers; then the king among his chief officers, heading the main divisions of cavalry, which covered many a broad acre, all mounted on strong horses; then followed large bodies of infantry intermingled with cavalry; and behind came the requirements of the camp, some borne on horseback, and a large portion on rude carriages drawn by oxen, mules, and horses. Of these the number seems to have been enormous, conveying as they did articles used in besieging castle or town, harness, victual, wine in cask and bottle, clothing and domestic utensils both for hall and chamber. The general impression seems to have been that the English would secure all Scotland to themselves, so that multitudes of the common people brought with them, as they best might, wife and child, pot and pan, pig and poultry.[10]

Among the crowd of travellers was one individual, Robert

---

[9] 'But king Edward and his people seemed rather to go towards a *wedding*, or a *triumph*, than to a battle, adorning themselves with all sorts of riches, gold, silver, and the like toyes, in a kind of wanton manner, correspondent to the humour of the prince whom they followed.'—*Speed*, p. 655

[10] 'And carriage men the quhilk war out of nummer,
  With wyfe and bairne, and mony laborous men,

Baston by name, a Carmelite friar of Scarborough, who being accounted a good Latin versifier, came by order of the king to celebrate in imperishable lines the conquest of Scotland. Whether on his way he stretched himself to rest at night beside the joiner and smith, like the two minstrels of Northumberland's Earl in the sixteenth century,[11] or he slept among better company, we have no means of knowing.

Through the whole course of the progress of King Edward on this expedition, he seems to have been so elevated by the enormous numbers of his army, that he firmly believed the Scots were unable to offer any resistance to his arms. The general conversation in almost every class was, how Scotland was to be disposed of, and it was arranged they would take Robert Bruce with his brother Edward, and convey them to London, to be dealt with as they deserved.[12] After this manner the King of England and his council spoke only of appropriating the plunder, so that Scotland might be divided among those of the army and others who were best deserving of such reward. In this case, according to the adage, they 'reckoned without the host,' for as our favourite author quaintly observes,—

'Or thai cum all to thair entent,
Howis in haile claith sall be rent.'

There can be no doubt that, with the view of resisting

Quhilk brocht with thame baith guiss, gryce and hen,
And houschald geir siclike as ilk man hed,
With all thair cleithing baith on bak and bed.'
*Stewart*, vol. iii. p. 222.

[11] *Northd. Book*, p. 390.

[12] 'The whole strength of England * * * produced such a confidence in every breast that the universal topic of conversation with this vast assemblage was not so much about carrying on the war, as about dividing the spoil.'—*Buchanan*, vol. i. p. 422.

the power of England, Robert Bruce had most carefully examined the whole vicinity of the way to Stirling, and, acquiring wisdom from the former battles in which he had been engaged, deemed it of the utmost importance to select a place most suitable to his purpose. Knowing the main object of King Edward was to press forward and relieve the castle there, he had to choose it in the likeliest line through which the English would attempt to pass, and prevent them reaching that fortress by any other route. Moreover, he had the privilege of causing the enemy to fight him on ground most advantageous to himself, and accordingly he fixed on the gentle slope of Bannockmoor,[13] so called by the common people at that time, for his battle-field, which was within the New Park, about two miles southward from Stirling. Here, however, it may be necessary to give the reader some account of the approach from Edinburgh to the latter place, and more particularly of the plot of land whereon the great conflict was decided.

We doubt not but considerable light might be thrown on the boundaries of New Park, could access be obtained to the charter-chests of the proprietors of the ground in that neighbourhood, or into the ancient records of the borough of Stirling. From the *Chamberlain's Accounts* we learn that, 'In 1263 the Sheriff of Stirling was employed in repairing the ancient park, and in constructing a new park there for Alexander III., and was allowed in his column of expenditure an outlay on that head of £80. Twenty years later there was an allowance for two park-keepers and one hunter of wolves at Stirling, and for the

---

[13] *Walsingham*, vol 1 p. 142  *Dugdale*, vol i. p 339.  *Carte*, vol ii. p 336

## LOCALITIES CONNECTED WITH THE BATTLE. 31

expenses of four hundred perches[14] of palisade round the new park; and for mowing and carrying hay and litter for the use of the fallow deer in winter.'[15] Again, Barbour relates that Sir Robert Clifford, when on his way to Stirling with his gallant troop of horse, *eschewit*[16] or avoided the New Park, wending his way onward beneath it, and also beneath the kirk, meaning that of St. Ninian's. Also the same author observes that when King Edward with his nobles betook themselves to flight on leaving Stirling, they *enweround*[17] or went round the Park in all haste towards Linlithgow. It would appear to have comprised a large tract of land, consisting of hill, dale, lake, and stream. Scotland's kings had kept it for the preservation of beasts of the chase, so that when they resided at Stirling they might enjoy the sports of the field either with falcon or hound. Wild animals found shelter in the higher uplands among the trees growing there, while the burn, the swamps, the wells, and their courses below, must have been the resort of water-fowl of every description. In all likelihood it included the mountain range round by Gillies' Hill, the land

---

[14] Twenty-two hundred yards.

[15] Quoted by Professor Cosmo Innes in *Scotland in the Middle Ages*, p. 125.

[16] 'The New Park all eschewit thai;
For thai wist weill the king wes thar;
And newth the New Park gan thai far,
Weill newth the kyrk, in till a rout.'
*Barbour*, p. 231.

[17] 'And be newth the castell went thai sone,
Rycht by the Round Table away:
And syne the Park enweround thai;
And towart Lythkow held in hy.'
*Barbour*, pp. 264-5.

chiefly covered with wood on each side of the Bannock for above a couple of miles, the Halbert and Milton Bogs, and in its eastern circuit, sweeping round the lower grounds, by the mills of Milton[18] towards the present town of Bannockburn, and near to the village of St. Ninian's. Probably the roads, if that by the Bore-stone was then formed, might be diverted round by its eastern extremity. We may likewise suppose that in 1314 the enclosures would be almost wholly broken down in the course of oppression which Scotland sustained from the first Edward, but within its limits, and especially on Bannockmoor, where the battle was to be fought, were portions of woodland, not a few, which Bruce considered would mar the charges of the English horse; and even at the present day the farm-steading erected on the lower portion of the field, where Walter the Steward and Sir James Douglas repelled the squadrons of the enemy, still bears the name of New Park.

The castle of Stirling was erected on the top of a lofty massive trap-rock, that rises abruptly from the level ground all round it, save on the south-east side, while on the north-east are some hilly eminences of lower elevation, but from these the castle is separated by the deep hollow of Ballangeich. On the north-west and north the sides of the rock are highest, presenting a series of lofty blocks of naked stone, rising almost perpendicularly above each other. Like the fortress at Edinburgh, the soil on its

---

[18] 'Bannocksborne, so named of oten-cakes called bannocks, which were used to bee made commonlie at the mils standing on the banks of the said water.'—*Hollinshed*, p. 217. Modern etymologists will say the word is derived from a different source than that ascribed to it by the old chronicler.

south-eastern side descends gradually from the summit down nearly to the level of the surrounding plain. Again, at a short distance from the bottom of this slope, a gentle rise takes place nearly southward, and, with some undulations, it continues about half-a-mile beyond St. Ninians, till the top of the height is reached near to the Bore-stone at Caldam Hill. Still farther east, towards the Whins of Milton, the rise continues, and behind this whole elevation, stretching from north-west to south-east, were Halbert's Bog and Milton Bog, the bottoms of which are now dry; but at an early period both formed, in all likelihood, one lake, which neither man nor horse could pass over.[19] Southward again from these sheets of water, Bannockburn, descending from the hills westward, flows down in an easterly direction to Milton, and on passing the mills there, bends northward, entering a deep ravine, which continues downward past the village bearing the name of the stream, till it winds through the level carse onward to the Forth.

The most direct route, therefore, from Falkirk to Stirling, by the only road apart from the broad carse, was over the piece of land between the lower end of Milton Bog and the head of the defile close to the village of Milton. The Roman road or street lay through this ground, which was only about five hundred yards in width, hence it was somewhat narrow for the passage of a large army, besides, the *lead* to the mills ran directly athwart it, and the Bannock had to be crossed, which ran amid moist boggy soil, the banks of which were high and broken. The other, and indeed the only remaining approach

---

[19] See Appendix. Note A.

for an army such as that of England, was higher up the stream, from the vicinity of Chartres Hall up to Park Mill, averaging a width of nearly half-a-mile, where the banks sloped to the burn, and where the latter could be easily passed over. Below the former place, the Bannock ran low among soil and slake,[20] while another broad morass or lake also stretched from its south-western margin to the rise of the ground immediately below Foot o' Green. Above Park Mill, again, the left bank of the burn, on looking downward, was almost impassable, not so much by rising abruptly from the stream to a considerable height, but from being covered northward, from the channel thereof to the high land overhanging it, with dense underwood and trees. Moreover, about a quarter of a mile above Park Mill, and in a northern direction, the Bannock descends from the west, forming nearly a right angle, for it rushes into and again flows down southward from the base of a lofty bank. It was from the rounded summit of this bank, down eastward in a gentle slope to the head of Halbert's Bog, measuring about eight hundred yards, where Bruce determined he should behold his warriors first strike for liberty.[21] Low down beneath him, on his right hand, hidden, yet giving forth notes of sweet melody among wood and bramble, the Bannock flowed to the south, while at a distance of above half-a-mile, away on his left, stretched the line of Halbert's and Milton bogs, gleaming with water.

---

[20] 'Bannokburne, that sua cumbyrsum was,
For slyk and depnes, for to pas,
That thar mycht nane out our it rid.'
*Barbour*, p. 264.

[21] Bruce 'posted himself . . . where he had a hill on his right flank, and a morass on his left.'—*Hume*, vol. iii. p. 18.

Before him the land descended, for nearly six hundred yards, gradually to the stream, which here wended again in an easterly direction, and on this plot of ground, nearly half-a-mile square, himself and his patriotic army had ultimately the good fortune to establish by arms the freedom and independence of Scotland.

Occupying this position, and knowing the sanguine anticipations of the King of England, Robert Bruce foresaw that if the enemy made no attempt to approach Stirling by the carse, which was unlikely, from the moistness of the soil, for portions of it might be under water, and thick underwood probably grew on and around it, but advanced by the main road, he would here await and take the fortune that God would send. One point he perceived must be dealt with, and that was to block up or render impassable the open space or thoroughfare at Milton, and if the road by the Bore-stone was then formed, to operate upon it in the same manner. Were either one or both open, a few troops of English horse might cross over, and not only throw succour into the castle of Stirling, but, while the Scottish forces were contending in battle, surround or attack them in flank or rear. Therefore, Bruce, believing himself, in the place he had selected, to be secure on the right, and thus defending his position on the left, the English must of necessity be compelled to meet his army face to face.[22] In this field he had ample room to bring into action the whole of his forces, and it was impossible his wings could be outflanked or surrounded by the enemy. The lines of his divisions might have been extended on

---

[22] 'The time and place were fixed by an obdurate necessity.'— *Burton*, vol. ii. p. 377.

a wider space, but if in any way they were confined, he had the sagacity to foresee that the English would be still more so, for not another opponent could enter into conflict than the front ranks who met his own spearmen.[23] Hereby the huge multitude of invaders who were behind would of course be crowded together in unwieldy masses, cumbering rather than taking part in the efficient movement of the whole.

---

[23] 'Battles are decided not by troops upon the muster rolls, nor even by those present, but by those alone who are simultaneously engaged. Numerical superiority of troops not engaged, so far from being useful, only increases the disorder.'—*Suppt. Encyclop. Britannica*, 1824, vol. vi. p. 760: article on 'War' by Major C. H. Smith.

## CHAPTER IV.

#### ADVANCE OF THE SCOTS TO NEW PARK.

*Stand fast and prepare thee; for the sword shall devour round about thee.*—JEREMIAH.

ON Friday the 21st June,[1] King Robert still lingering in the Torwood, went through and most carefully examined his whole army, speaking to those near him words of great kindness, in the full assurance that when the approaching struggle came their efforts would be crowned with success.[2] To the chief officers who formed his privy council he communicated his arrangement for battle. He first pointed out the great importance of preventing any detachment of

---

[1] In 1314 Midsummer day fell on Monday the 24th of June, being that of the nativity of St. John the Baptist.

[2] 'The king has sene all thair hawing,
And knew him weile in to sic thing;
And saw thaim all commounaly
Off sic contenance, and sa hardy,
For owt effray or abaysing,
In his hart had he gret liking.
And thoucht that men of sa gret will,
Giff thai wald set thair will thar till,
Suld be full hard to wyn perfay.
And as he met thaim in the way,
He welcummyt thaim with glaidsum far,
Spekand gud wordis her and thar.'

*Barbour*, pp. 222-3.

the enemy moving forward to the aid of Stirling Castle.[3] Next he observed that when the thoroughfare at Milton was closed, the English, on their approach, must needs advance about half-a-mile farther up on the south-west side of the Bannock, till they crossed it, where they would be encountered at great advantage. The Scottish force they knew amounted to above thirty thousand fighting men, and if these were separated into four divisions, should their enemies attempt to pass over or near the morass, which, if it were possible, could only be done either singly or by a limited number at once, they would be met and readily overcome.[4] Moreover, he deemed it exceedingly desirable that they should go lightly armed on foot to battle, for the English, being more powerful, rode better horses, and did

---

[3] "Lordis, now ye see
'That Inglis men, with mekill mycht,
'Has all disponyt thaim for the fycht,
'For thai yone castell wald reskew.
'Tharfor is gud we ordane now
'How we may let* thaim of thair purpos,
'And sua to thaim the wayis closs,
'That thai pass nocht, but gret letting."
　　　　　　　　　　*Barbour*, p. 223.

[4] "We haiff her with ws at bidding
'Weile thretty thowsand men, and ma.
'Mak we four bataillis of tha,
'And ordane ws on sic maner,
'That when our fayis cummys ner,
'We to the New Park hald our way,
'For thar behowys thaim nede away,
'But giff that they will be newth us ga,
'And our the merraiss passand swa,
'We sall be at awantage thar."
　　　　　　　　　　*Barbour*, p 223.

---

\* *Let*—present.

the Scots attempt to encounter them with cavalry, the result might be attended with great peril. Therefore, if they fought on foot, they could take advantage of the ground, for several clumps of trees were on Bannockmoor, which, with the open swamps and watercourses below,[5] would cumber and put their assailants to great perplexity.[6] To these suggestions the leaders readily agreed, while Bruce knew well the importance of availing himself of their counsel on every case of emergency. Of the four companies into which it was proposed the army should be portioned, the van or central division[7] in the line of battle, they com-

---

[5] In all probability the margins of the lake or lakes of Halbert and Milton Bogs, together with the grounds through which Bannockburn flowed near to Milton, were soft and spongy. From the drainage and improvement of land which has taken place within the last century, we of the present day can scarcely form an idea of the number of 'joggle-beds,' 'well-eyes,' and quagmires, which existed all over the land in former times. An old man told the author many years ago, that in early life he lived on a small farm in an upland district, and almost every other day, during summer, it was necessary to have a couple of horses and ropes at hand to drag out some young cow or horse, which, in seeking the fresh grass, had sunk in one of these places, and was of itself unable to get out.

[6] "And gyff we fecht on fute, perfay
'At a wantage we sall be ay.
'For in the park, amang the treys,
'The horss men [cumbryt beis] alwayis.
'And the sykis als sua, that ar thar doun,
'Sall put thaim to confusioune."
*Barbour*, p. 224.

[7] Barbour and the chroniclers, who have written on the great struggle at Bannockburn, seemed to have considered the central division usually formed the van of an army in battle. It was intended

mitted to the leadership of Randolph Earl Moray, whose troops were drawn probably from the lands bordering on the Moray Firth, and from the valleys of Nairn, Findhorn, and the rapid Spey. Beneath his banner several of the lords and chief men of the kingdom were stationed.[8] The right wing was intrusted to the guidance of Sir Edward Bruce, whose bravery in every instance merited the highest praise, for our venerable chronicler graphically observes that whatever the result of the conflict might be, his opponents would have ample cause of lamentation.[9] His forces, brave almost as himself, were likely brought from those parts of Scotland which lay beyond the influence of his martial brethren in arms. On young Walter

---

so in this field, but in several other battles, including those of Neville's Cross and Agincourt on the side of England, the right wing, as has been already stated, had the honour of forming the van.

[8] 'Thair four bataillis ordanyt thai,
And till the erle Thomas perfay
Thai gaif the waward in leding;
For in his noble gouernyng,
And in his hey chewalry,
Thai assoweryt rycht soueranly.
And, for to maynteyme his baner,
Lordis, that of gret worschip wer,
War assygnyt, with thair mengné,
In till his battaill for to be.'
*Barbour*, p. 224.

[9] 'The tothyr bataill was gevyn to led
Till him, that douchty wes of deid,
And prisyt off hey chewalry;
That wes Schyr Eduuard the worthy.
I trow he sall maynteyme it sua
That, howsa euir the gamyn ga,
His fayis to plenye sall mater haf.'
*Barbour*, p. 224.

the Steward, and James Douglas, devolved the command of the left wing, the former having been instructed in warfare by the latter—a proven warrior—and this body consisted chiefly of tried Border warriors, accustomed from childhood to the use of battle-axe and spear, together with about one-third part of mountaineers from the north of Scotland.[10] The fourth and last section of the army, Robert Bruce designed to take under his own charge, and these were his tried men of Carrick, of Argyle, Angus Lord of Kintyre and the Isles, with a large number from the plain land.[11] Those, therefore, with the King were to

---

[10] 'And syne the thrid bataill thai gaff
Till Waltre Stewart for to leid ;
And to Douglas douchty of deid.
Thai war cosyngis in ner degre,
Tharfor till him betaucht wes he :
For he wes young ; but nocht for thi
I trow he sall sa manlily
Do his dewour, and wirk sa weill,
That him sall nede ne mar yemseill.'
Barbour, pp. 224-5.

[11] 'The ferd bataile the noble king
Tuk till his awne gouernyng :
And had in till his cumpany
The men of Carrik halely ;
And off Arghile, and of Kentyr,
And off the Ilis, quharoff wes Syr
Anguss of Ile and But, all tha.
He of the plane land had alsua
Off armyt men a mekill rout :
His bataill stalwart wes and stout.
He said the rerward he wald ma ;
And ewyn [be] for him suld ga
The waward ; and, on athir hand,
The tothyr bataillis suld be gangand,

form the rearward, and from the elevated ground which they afterwards occupied, they must have been stationed behind Sir Edward Bruce and Randolph, ready to give help where it was required. In addition to the said divisions of troops, a large number of archers were also to be placed ready for battle, and above five hundred cavalry were to be at hand, that their force might be applied where it was most effective. These horsemen the King had especially appointed to perform a certain exploit, which will be related hereafter.

Robert Bruce, availing himself of the wisdom and experience of the chief men around him, made every arrangement for battle. Next day being Saturday, the 22d June, on learning by his scouts that the English had come to Edinburgh and passed the night there, he gave orders that the whole army should move on towards Bannockmoor, which they did by the Roman road that led through

---

>     Besid on sid a litill space :
>     And the king, that behind thaim was,
>     Suld se quhar thar war mast myster,
>     And releve thar with his baner.'—*Barbour*, p. 225.

'Angus M'Donald, Lord of the Isles and Kintyre, in 1306 received Bruce into his castle of Dunaverty, and protected him for nine months in his country of Rachlin, Isla, and Uist. In consequence of this never-to-be-forgotten fidelity, the King bestowed upon him as a reward the honour of taking the *right hand* in the battle of Bannockburn. His clan enjoyed this privilege from that time, with exception of the battle of Harlaw in 1411, when it was given to the Laird M'Clean, and that of Culloden, but they took their position on the right both at Gladsmuir and Falkirk.'—*Lockhart Papers*, vol. ii. p. 510. This gallant chieftain, with his followers, must either have remained with the King, and fought in his presence during the battle, or taken his place on the right side of the warriors led by Sir Edward Bruce.

## ADVANCE OF THE SCOTS TO NEW PARK. 43

the Torwood onward to the north, and lay a little to the west of Stirling.[12] This causeway descended in a straight line from the west side of the farm-steadings of Snabhead and Pirnhall, crossed the Bannock, passed within a short distance east of the Bore-stone, and continued through the hollow on a part of the road between Coxet Hill and St. Ninians. But, as has been stated, a part of it from near Milton to the latter place was probably comprised within the New Park, and though the fences thereof might be destroyed, the locality would still retain the same name. Accordingly, when the army came to Milton, the King caused a number of active men, accustomed to the spade in agriculture, to dig a series of deep pits, close together like a honeycomb, across the neck of land from the lower end of Milton Bog to the lofty banks of the burn below that village.[13] Both the ancient Roman way, and pro-

---

[12] ' And on the morn, on Settreday,
  The king hard his discourouris say
  That Inglis men, with mekill mycht,
  Had lyin at Edinburgh all nycht.
  Tharfor, with owtyn mar delay,
  He till the New Park held his way,
  With all that in his leding war ;
  And in the park thaim herberyt thar.'
  *Barbour*, pp. 225-6.

[13] ' And in a plane feld, be the way,
  Quhar he thoucht ned behowyd away
  The Inglis men, gif that thai wald
  Throw the park to the castell hald,
  He gert men mony pottis ma,
  Off a fute breid round ; and all tha
  War dep wp till a mannys kne ;
  Sa thyk, that thai mycht liknyt be
  Till a wax cayme, that beis mais.'—*Barbour*, p. 226.

bably a more recent road, which may have been made to the east of the New Park when it was enclosed, were thus cut through, that all passage thereon, or near them, might be prevented. When those pitfalls were excavated, Bruce ordered them to be covered first with branches of trees, and above these green turf to be laid, and the earth so scattered about as not to show where the hollows really were.[14] If the road at Brock's Brae was then formed, we may presume it was broken up, and the pits concealed in the same manner. Had these cavities been left open, the reader will perceive how easily the English might have caused them to be filled up, so that no obstacle then could have prevented them passing over. The Scots were occupied in digging them all night, and had them completed next morning.

---

Barbour's words 'be the way' can have only two meanings. One may be that the pots were dug in a plain field, close by the *way* whereon Bruce and his army went to the New Park. The other may signify that the plain field was near the Roman *way*, or old road, which was undoubtedly observable through the whole district at that early date. If any critic can elicit another meaning from the expression, I shall be glad to know it. Besides, the holes were made for the express purpose of preventing the enemy going through the Park to the Castle.

[14] It is improbable that Bruce, by the aid even of his chaplain, ever had *Herodotus* translated to him; but that author relates an incident almost similar to what was practised by the Scottish King. 'There is,' says he, 'a pass near the city of Hyampolis, where the Phocians, having dug a broad trench, filled up the void with empty wine-jars, after which they covered the place with mould, so that the ground all looked alike, and then awaited the coming of the Thessalians. These, thinking to destroy the Phocians at one sweep, rushed rapidly forward, and became entangled in the wine-jars, which broke the legs of their horses.'—*Herodotus*, vol. iv. p. 287.

## ADVANCE OF THE SCOTS TO NEW PARK.

About this time we may conclude the Scottish army occupied the height from the Whins of Milton to Caldam Hill, with the hollow west of it, up to Coxet Hill, and if the staff of the royal standard of Scotland was ever planted in the Bore-stone, the broad folds of that banner must have waved from it during that Saturday afternoon.[15] A few troops might be placed on the spot selected for battle, which was soon to be trodden down and flowing with human blood, but Bruce, we suspect, had the sense to leave that as it were open, till he saw the English advance, and if they took possession of the opposite ground near Foot o' Green and its vicinity, all would appear favourable. Still he was uncertain by what way or in what order they would approach, so that he could only hold his own army in readiness to meet them, and guard the passage to the fortress of Stirling. He took no rest during the night,[16] but wandered about from one portion of his army to another, revolving in his mind the circumstances in which he was placed, and the bearing they might have on the future of Scotland, yet providing for all that might occur, and trusting to a higher power than that of man, so that when the shock of battle came these heroic men around him might be enabled eventually to achieve the freedom of their native land.

---

[15] See Appendix. Note B.
[16] 'All that nycht trawailland he wais.'
*Barbour*, p. 226.

## CHAPTER V.

### COMMENCEMENT OF HOSTILITIES.

Robert the Bruce
With threttie thousand worthie men and wycht
In the prospect of King Edward richt playne
On ane fair feild richt equall him forgaue,
Planetit his palzeonis pertlie in the tyde,
And baldlie thair schupe to remane and byde.
STEWART.

NEXT morning, on Sunday, the 23d of June, not long after the sun arose, the whole army of Scotland were collected, and they heard mass, which was celebrated in suitable order by the clergy who were present. Many confessed their sins most devoutly, and made solemn preparation either to offer up their lives in the impending struggle, or free their land from a foreign yoke. To the Most High earnest prayers were put up for assistance, and, as the result proved, these orisons happily were not offered in vain. The day, be it remembered, preceded that of St. John the Baptist, and as the stern reality of battle was at hand they all fasted, resigning themselves to the keeping of their Maker, and allaying hunger on a little bread and water.[1] We who have come after, and enjoy, to the

---

[1] 'On Sonday than, in the mornyng,
Weile sone eftir the sone rising,
Thai hard thair mess commounaly.
And mony thaim schraiff full devotly,
That thought to dey in that mellé,

fullest extent, all the blessings of liberty, ought ever to be most thankful to God, and not less grateful to the memory of our glorious ancestors, who, in the face of privation and death, nobly won us that inheritance, which, under the auspices of heaven, we and our successors shall always be enabled resolutely to maintain. When the solemnity performed by the priests was over, the King went and examined the pits which were then completed, and saw them on each side of the way done to his approval.[2] He was convinced that if any troop of horsemen attempted to force

---

Or than to mak thair contré fre.<br>
To God, for thair rycht, prayit thai.<br>
Thar dynit nane of thaim that day ;<br>
Bot, for the vigil of Sanct Jhane,<br>
Thai fastyt water and breid ilkan.'<br>
Barbour, p. 226.

[2] 'The King, quhen that the mess wes don,
Went furth to se the pottis sone ;
And at his liking saw thaim mad.
On athir sid, rycht weill braid,
It wes pittyt, as Ik haif tauld.
Giff that thair fayis on horss wald hald
Furth in that way, I trow thai sall
Nocht weill eschaip for owtyn a fall.'
*Barbour*, pp. 226-7.

The above extract furnishes another proof that the pits were not dug in the battle-field; and our old bard carefully repeats the remark that they were excavated to prevent the English horsemen going forth in 'that way' towards Stirling. Of the two meanings the words can possibly have, as cited in the note at p. 44, the latter, from the above lines, is evidently to be preferred, namely, that it was the Roman *way* the author signified, since the holes were made not only upon it, but on either side of it, for the purpose already stated. The expression seems clear as any passage whatever in our poet's volume.

a passage in this direction, they would find the undertaking more difficult than they at first contemplated.

But the time drawing near when the English would approach, King Robert, by way of showing his army the exact order of battle, and the ground they were to occupy, gave orders they should arm themselves speedily, and he led them to the locality he had selected, on which their valour was shortly to be put to the proof. Wending round the northern verge of Halbert's Bog, and ascending to the west in the direction of the northern angle of Bannockburn, above Park Mill and towards Graystale, each division in lines came to occupy the position on which they were to meet the enemy; and this was done that no confusion might ensue when the eventful hour of conflict arrived.[3] And now King Robert, with the design of rendering his cause most popular, ordered proclamation to be made that of all the fighting men assembled there, whoever feared his heart would fail him in the ensuing struggle, and who had not resolved either to win all or die with honour, was at liberty to quit the ranks instantly and depart home.[4]

---

[3] 'Throw out the ost than gert he cry
That all suld arm thaim hastily,
And busk thaim on thair best maner.
And quhen thai assemblyt wer,
He gert aray thaim for the fycht.'
*Barbour*, p. 227.

[4] 'And syne gert cry our all on hycht,
That quha sa euir he war, that fand
Hys hart nocht sekyr for to stand
To wyn all, or dey with honur,
For to maynteyme that stalwart stour,
That he betyme suld hald his way;
And [nane] suld duell with him, bot thai

He wished only, he observed, to have true and gallant heroes with him, who would do their utmost for the welfare of Scotland, and remain with him throughout the crisis, to take the fortune that God would vouchsafe to the noble and the brave. On this being known, a loud shout of exultation arose from the whole army, and the general cry was that none should fail, but remain firm to the last, in order to achieve the liberty of their country.[5]

Hereupon the King enjoyed great satisfaction, being convinced he could place the utmost dependence on the bravery and patriotism of his men.[6] Apart from the regular army above mentioned, there were nearly twenty thousand of men, women, and grown-up lads, who had charge of victual, harness, and other necessary articles, and who followed the camp on every occasion. These,

---

That wald stand with him to the end,
And tak the vre that God wald send.'
Barbour, p. 227.

[5] 'Than all ansuerd with a cry,
And with a woce said generaly;
That nane for dout off deid suld faile,
Quhill discumfyt war the gret bataile.'
Barbour, p. 227.

[6] 'Quhen the gud king has hard his men
Sa hardely ansuer him then,
Sayand that nothyr dede, na dreid,
Till sic discomfort suld thaim leid,
That thai suld eschew the fechting;
In hart he had gret reiosing.
For him thoucht men off sic covyne,
Sa gud and hardy, and sa fyne.
Suld weile in bataill hald thair rycht,
Agayne men off full mekill mycht.'
Barbour, p. 227.

with the stores for general use, were sent away to the west, up what is now called Gillie's Hill,[7] to a small valley leading northward to the higher ground there, in order to be concealed from the view of the English, and with these, we are inclined to suppose, Bruce had also an especial purpose to perform.[8]

When the King had thus placed his army in due order of battle, he learned that on the previous night, that of Saturday, the English had advanced to Falkirk, and were coming straight onward to Stirling.[9] Accordingly, we suspect, the several battalions withdrew from line and shifted position, but were ready to form again whenever it was necessary.[10] They chiefly fell back in the direction of

---

[7] *Gillie*, a male servant.

[8] 'Syne all the smale folk, and pitall,
He send with harnays and with wictaill
In till the park, weill fer him fra;
And fra the bataillis gert thaim ga.
And as he bad, thai went thar way;
Twenty thowsand weile ner war thai.
Thai held thair way till a walé.'—*Barbour*, pp. 227-8.

[9] 'The king left with a clene mengné.
The quethir thai war thretty thousand,
That I trow sall stalwartly stand,
And do thair dewour as thai aw.
Thai stud than rangyt all on raw,
Redy for to gyff hard battaill,
Giff ony folk wald thaim assaile.'—*Barbour*, p. 228.

[10] 'The king gert thaim all buskit be;
For he wyst in certanté
That his fayis all nycht lay
At the Fawkyrk; and syne that thai
Held towart him the way all straucht,
With mony men of mekill maucht.'—*Barbour*, p. 228.

St. Ninians, and Bruce, in order to prevent the English from throwing by stratagem any succour into Stirling Castle, notwithstanding the precaution already taken of digging the pits, appointed Randolph, with a sufficient force, to keep the way near to the Kirk, at the former place.[11] He observed that himself and his brother, with the Steward, would prevent them approaching in any other direction.[12]

It was an anxious time for Bruce, for he despatched James Douglas and Sir Robert Keith Marischal, to observe the appearance of the English, so that, taking a few horse with them, they advanced in the direction of the Torwood, and very soon came in view of the enemy.[13] To these warriors it was a splendid and magnificent sight. In every direction to the south-east, so far as the openings amid trees extended, shields, helmets, and lances innumerable,

---

[11] 'Tharfor till his newo bad he,
The erle off Murreff, with his menye,
Besid the kyrk to kepe the way,
That na man pass that gat away,
For to debate the castell.
And he said, him self suld weill
Kep the entré with his bataill,
Giff that ony wald thar assale.'—*Barbour*, p. 228.

[12] We have here additional proof that Robert Bruce expected the English, on their way to Stirling, would pass either upon or near the Roman road. His care to have the pits dug at Milton points to the same conclusion. The said way, as has been stated, held its course a little to the west of the kirk and village of St. Ninians.

[13] 'The king send than James of Douglas,
And Schyr Robert the Keyth, that than was
Marschell off all the ost, of fé,
The Inglis mennys come to se.'—*Barbour*, pp. 228-9.

were everywhere sparkling in the rays of the sun—banners, standards, and the pennons attached to whole forests of spears, waved in the breeze. The gorgeous and rich dresses in almost every bright colour, worn by countless knights, were dazzling to behold, while squadrons beyond counting, on horse and foot, far as the eye could discern, might suffice to impress with awe the most mighty power in Christendom.[14] Douglas and Keith thereupon rode back to the King, and on telling him of the beauty, the splendour, and the gorgeous equipment of the English in untold numbers, he cautioned them not to divulge what they had witnessed, but to intimate that the foe, though numerous, approached in the utmost disorder. Bruce well knew it was necessary to put the best construction on the tidings, giving the army, by his looks and manner, perfect assurance that all would be well; and they also, apart from the justice of their cause, having implicit confidence in his ability as a leader, concluded that whatever opposition they might

---

[14] ' And sone the gret ost haf thai sene,
Quhar scheildis schynand war sa schene,
And bassynetis burnyst brycht,
That gave agayne the sone gret lycht.
Thai saw sa fele browdyne baneris,
Standaris, and pennownys, and speris,
And sa fele knychtis apon stedis,
All flawmand in thair [joly] wedis;
And sa fele bataillis, and sa braid,
That tuk sa gret rowme as thai raid,
That the maist ost, and the stoutest,
Off Crystyndome, and the grettest,
Suld be abaysit for to se
Thair fayis in to sic quantité,
And swa arayit for to fycht.'—*Barbour*, p. 229.

encounter, the struggle would eventually terminate in their favour. At this time we may suppose, that while waiting the advance of the English, and ready to do battle with them, the Scottish forces were ranged not only on the battlefield, but on the height near the Bore-stone, the cavalry were at hand, and the King himself being on horseback, in company with one or two of his leaders, that he might observe every hostile movement, whether from the south or east, occupied the summit of Coxet Hill.

Soon afterwards the waving banners of the English were descried on the heights near Plean, and behind Snabhead, and as they advanced and saw the Scots occupying the New Park, the chief leaders consulted together, and determined, if possible, to relieve the castle of Stirling. To accomplish this enterprise, they selected a troop of eight hundred horsemen, youthful and brave, who ardently aspired to distinguish themselves, and these, in charge of three barons accustomed to arms, among whom was Henry Beaumont,[15] were arrayed under command of Sir Robert Clifford, a tried warrior.[16] They saw many bat-

---

[15] *Lel. Coll.*, vol. ii. p. 546.

[16] ' The Inglis men, in sic aray
As ye haf herd me forouth say,
Come with thair bataillis approchand,
The baneris to the wynd wawand.
And quhen thai cummyn war sa ner,
That bot twa myle betuix thaim wer,
Thai chesyt a joly cumpany
Off men, that wicht war and hardy,
On fayr courseris armyt at rycht.
Four lordys off mekill mycht
War capitanis of that route.
The Syr the Clyffurd, that wes stout,

talions of the Scots arrayed both on the ground selected for battle, and on the height west of the Whins of Milton, but suspecting that Bruce was there, the troop of horse under Clifford, hid from view by trees which grew on the low ground between them and Milton, threaded their way either near to the spot whereon the present bridge stands, or by the little valley in front of Craigford, and diving into the defile, swept past the place on which the house of Hill Park stands, and, favoured by the rising ground on the left, held on unobserved beneath the New Park direct for Stirling.[17] Advancing, however, below the church of St. Ninians, Clifford's horse came more into view, and the eagle-eye of Bruce detecting them, he gave orders for the Scottish cavalry to advance, and riding forward to Randolph, who was on the lower ground, told him he had permitted the enemy to pass, observing in the symbolic language of chivalry that 'a rose had fallen from his chaplet.'[18]

> Wes off thaim all souerane leidar:
> Aucht hundre armyt, I trow, thai war.
> Thai war all young men, and joly,
> Yarnand to do chewalry;
> Off best of ywill the ost war thai
> Off contenance, and off aray.'
> *Barbour*, pp. 230-1.

[17] See Note 16, p. 31, *supra*.

[18] A chaplet is a string of beads used by Roman Catholics in reciting the Lord's prayer, etc., and Lord Hailes imagines that *rose* implies the large bead therein for distinguishing a *Pater Noster* from an *Ave Maria.*—*Annals*, vol. ii. p. 44, note. The phrase, we suspect, is less involved. Randolph, by his bravery, had gained distinction, and the king likened this to a chaplet of flowers for the hero's brow, among which roses were intertwined—hence, probably, the allusion.

By this time Clifford's troop had advanced so far as to be between Randolph and Stirling, and as it was impossible for infantry to overtake them, the latter leader headed the Scottish horse, and led them instantly in pursuit.[19] Clifford, perceiving the Scots behind him, caused his horsemen to wheel round and give them battle.[20]

---

[19] 'The erle Thomas, that wes sa stout,
Quhen he saw thaim sa ta the plane,
In gret hy went he thaim agane,
With fyve hundre, for owtyn ma,
Anoyit in his hart, and wa
That thai sa fer wer passit by.
For the king haid said him rudly,
That ' a rose of his chaplete
' Was fallyn ;' for quhar he wes set
To kep the way thai men war past.'
*Barbour*, p. 231.

[20] Among the authorities who say that Randolph took cavalry with him are these :—*Buchanan*, vol. i. p. 424 ; *Hollinshed*, p. 217; *Godscroft*, p. 32. Also *Nisbet*, in his account of the family of Keith, vol. ii., appendix, p. 4, says—' At the battle of Bannockburn he (Sir Robert Keith) commanded 500 horse, and gave the first onset, and defeat a party of English horse sent to reinforce Philip Mowbray, governor of Stirling, which made way for that glorious victory King Robert obtained in the above mentioned place.' Others, even down to the present day, including Tytler, Scott (Hist. of Scotland), and Taylor, tell us they were spearmen or infantry. Barbour, in relating the circumstance, says the English were ' on fair coursers,' and that Randolph went against them with ' five hundred,' whereby he might mean horse without expressly saying so. Many historians follow their predecessors without thinking on the subject they are handling, and the following points deserve investigation. Is it likely that a body of men on foot could overtake a troop of cavalry who had passed by to some distance ere they were pursued? What probability is there that the five hundred horsemen with Bruce remained idle when a

We are unable to say whether Randolph ordered his men to dismount and fight on foot, placing their horses behind them, or to meet the enemy in the saddle, but he caused them to form a circle and draw up side by side, with their spears protruding outward, and thus withstand the assault of the foe.[21] The shock was serious; Sir William Daynecourt, being first in the onset, was instantly slain. The others came on more leisurely, and attempted

circumstance of this kind occurred, for which they were specially adapted? Besides the perspiration, the breath, and the dust which, according to Barbour, arose in the midst of men and horse during the conflict, was it possible, as we learn afterwards, that footmen could outstrip and cut down those mounted English who, when defeated, were last in the flight? The whole achievement, from whatever point it may be seen, must, of course, come within the limits of probability.

[21] ' And quhen the erle saw that menye
Cum sa stoutly, till his said he ;
' Be nocht abaysit for thair schor,
' Bot settis speris yow befor.
' And bak to bak set all your rout
' And all the speris poyntis owt.
' Swagate ws best defend may we,
' Enweronyt with thaim gif we be.'
And as he bad thaim thai haf done.'
*Barbour*, p. 232.

The spot where this memorable conflict took place is still called 'Randolph's Field,' and is situated half-way between St. Ninians and Stirling, on the west side of the turnpike road. This proves the English had advanced to a considerable distance ere they were overtaken by the Scots. Fortunately, the place is marked by two large upright stones, which had been set up as memorials of Randolph's victory over Clifford's troop. We have, therefore, cause of regret that the site of the later and still more glorious battlefield was not indicated to future ages by some enduring landmarks of the same kind.

time after time to break through the barrier of Scottish lances, but always with a loss to themselves. It seemed marvellous how the defensive band maintained its position, surrounded by such heavy-armed assailants; still they did so, and acquitted themselves most bravely. No impression could be made upon them, while the horses of the English, as they neared the fatal ring, being pierced probably by the longer weapons of the Scots, reared and threw their riders, who were trampled under foot and destroyed.[22] Some again of the Scots, when opportunity occurred, broke forward from their fellows, and dealing deadly blows both on horse and man, fell backward again to complete the defensive line of opposing steel.[23] When the English perceived they could not break through the front of these northern warriors, they threw among them, with the utmost fury, maces, swords, and daggers, till the very weapons were piled above each other.[24] As the struggle continued, the day being warm, the perspiration poured out over men and horses, and the dust arose above them like clouds at every fresh attempt to dash through the impenetrable

---

[22] 'And thai with speris woundis wyd
Gaff till the horss that cum thaim ner:
And thai that ridand on thaim wer,
That doune war borne, losyt the lyvis.'
*Barbour*, pp. 232-3.

[23] 'For sum wald schout out of thair rout,
And off thaim that assaylyt about,
Stekyt stedis, and bar doun men.'—*Barbour*, p. 233.

[24] 'The Inglis men sa rudly then
Kest amang thaim suerdis and mass,
That ymyd thaim a monteyle was
Of wapynnys, that war warpyt thar.'
*Barbour*, p. 233.

circle.[25] Yet not a man gave way, and every onset only occasioned additional loss to the English. The desperate struggle was intently observed by Bruce, one or two of whose chief leaders were near him, and at last, seeing no chance for Randolph in the midst of such an array, Douglas, though these heroes at that instant were not on terms of intimate friendship,[26] besought the King that he might take a number of men and render his fellow-officer assistance. 'You shall not move,' said Bruce, 'for I will not alter my order of battle; let Randolph acquit himself as he best may.'[27] 'I cannot stand here and see him overcome,' observed Douglas, 'so with your leave I must aid him whatever befall.' 'Go then,' said the King, 'but return speedily, for even now I require all the assistance I can command.' Douglas thereupon departed, taking with

---

[25] 'On athir half thai war sa stad,
For the rycht gret heyt that thai had,
For fechtyn, and for sonnys het,
That all thair flesche of swate wes wete.
And sic a stew raiss out of thaim then,
Off aneding bath of hors and men,
And off powdyr; that sic myrknes
In till the ayr abowyne thaim wes,
That it wes wondre for to se'—*Barbour*, p 233

[26] 'Suppois that tyme that he and he wes fais.'
*Stewart*, vol. iii. p. 226.

[27] 'The king said; 'Sa our Lord me se!
'A fute till him thow sall nocht ga
'Giff he weile dois, lat him weile ta.
'Quhethir euir him happyn to win or loss,
'I will nocht for him brek purpos.''
*Barbour*, p 234.

We have here ample proof how Bruce considered order as most essential to be observed in battle array.

## COMMENCEMENT OF HOSTILITIES.

him a number of infantry, but observing, as he approached the conflict, that the English were in confusion, and on the point of defeat, for many saddles were empty, he forbore to advance farther, saying, 'The Earl of Moray is about to overcome the enemy, and we must not presume to share in his well-earned glory. Let us return to the King, for he requires our help!' Then without delay he withdrew the men towards the main army.[28]

---

[28] 'James of Dowglas, be thair relying,
　　Knew that thai war discumfyt ner:
　　Than bad thaim, that with him wer,
　　Stand still, and press na forthyrmar.'
　　　　　　　　　　　　*Barbour,* p. 238.

## CHAPTER VI.

### SIR HENRY DE BOHUN KILLED.

In God's name, cheerly on, courageous friends,
To reap the harvest of perpetual peace
By this one bloody trial of sharp war.
                                    SHAKESPEARE

DOUGLAS had spoken the truth, for Robert Bruce, on observing that the English army was advancing in a north-western direction, gave orders that his own troops should move forward and occupy the ground he had specially selected for them. King Edward, when he came near to Snabhead, must have tarried for a time among his chief men, and observed not only the castle of Stirling, which stood full in view on its summit of rock, but marked the several divisions of the Scots, for he could scarcely believe, on considering his own enormous strength, that they would have the assurance to oppose him in actual conflict. Besides, only a portion of his forces must have come up, for they would occupy miles of road, and his carriages and waggons were still moving westward nearly all the way from Falkirk. Nor is it improbable that another squadron of his cavalry, by way of trying the lines of approach, ventured to force a passage by Milton, and found it ineffectual. Forward, however, moved the army, till at length King Edward had himself probably come to the sloping ground near to Foot o' Green, when he ordered a halt to be made, in order that he might take counsel with his leaders[1] whether they would rest that night to recruit the strength of the troops, or go forward and instantly commence the battle. The Earls of Gloucester[2] and Hereford, who led the van, not being aware of the command to halt, led on their squadrons of horse till they crossed the Bannock and ascended the acclivity in the direction of the Scottish lines.[3] Robert Bruce, in the absence of Randolph, had marshalled his battalions, as has been stated, on the space they were to occupy, and being mounted on a small but active horse, he rode along the front of his divisions fully armed, wearing a light crown of gold on his basinet, and having a battle-axe in his hand.[4] Not expecting any

---

[1] '. . . The king off Ingland, quhen he
　　Was cummyn with his gret menyc
　　Ner to the place, as I said ar,
　　Quhar Scottis men arayit war,
　　He gert arest all his bataill,
　　And othyr alsua to tak consaill,
　　Quhethir thai wald herbry thaim that nycht;
　　Or than but mar ga to the fycht.'—*Barbour*, p. 235.

[2] Gloucester rode a beautiful horse, a present from the King, who received it as a gift from Richard Kellow, Bishop of Durham.

[3] 'The waward, that wist na thing
　　Off this arest, na his duelling,
　　Raid to the Park all straucht thair way,
　　For owtyn stinting, in gud aray.'—*Barbour*, p. 235.

[4] 'And quhen the king wist that thai wer,
　　In hale bataill, cummand sa ner,
　　His bataill gert he weill aray.
　　He raid apon a litill palfray,
　　Laucht; and joly arayand
　　His bataill, with an ax in hand.
　　And on his bassynet he bar
　　An hat off tyre aboune ay quhar;
　　And thar wpon, in to taknyng,
　　Ane hey croune, that he wes king.'—*Barbour*, p. 235.

immediate assault, he spoke words of comfort to his soldiers; and, to those near him, gave every assurance of victory. By this time it is likely the foremost of the English horse had approached to within a short distance from Bruce, when a valiant knight, Sir Henry Bohun, who was cousin to the Earl of Hereford, observing King Robert aloof from his troops, and being ambitious of accomplishing a notable feat of arms, spurred his war-horse toward him, supposing he might either kill him or take him prisoner. When the heroic King, who had come off unscathed from many encounters of this kind, saw him make the attempt, the spirit of the old Adam so roused his heart and braced his nerves that he met him in the shock, but turning his horse slightly to the left, he parried the point of De Bohun's lance, and swinging his axe round, with a tremendous blow, crashed the helmet and brain of his opponent, laying him dead among his charger's feet.[5]

---

[5] 'And quhen Schyr Henry saw the king
Cum on, for owtyn abaysing,
Till him he raid in full gret hy.
He thoucht that he suld weill lychtly
Wyn him, and haf him at his will,
Sen he him horsyt saw sa ill.
Sprent thai samyn in till a ling.
Schyr Henry myssit the noble king
And he, that in his sterapys stud,
With the ax that wes hard and gud,
With sa gret mayne raucht him a dynt,
That nothyr hat, na helm, mycht stynt
The hewy dusche that he him gave,
That ner the heid till the harnys clave.
The hand ax schaft fruschit in twa,
And he doune to the erd gan ga
All flatlynys, for him faillyt mycht.'—*Barbour*, p. 236

In the haste and heat of the moment, though the edge of the steel effectually accomplished the King's purpose, the stroke had been dealt somewhat obliquely, for the shaft of the weapon was broken in his grasp. This passage of arms was witnessed by both armies, and accordingly the front ranks of the Scots took heart, and, raising a great shout, advanced with their spears before them, but the English withdrew, being dismayed on observing their daring adventurer so speedily overcome, though a few were overtaken and killed.[6] On recalling the Scottish pursuers, the chief men around the King blamed him for putting his life in jeopardy when the battle had yet to be struck; but he, fully aware of the importance of the charge, turned it aside by expressing his sorrow that he had shivered the handle of his good battle-axe.[7]

By this time the Earl of Moray had succeeded in van-

---

[6] 'And quhen the kingis men thaim saw
Swa in hale bataill thaim withdraw,
A gret schout till thaim gan thai mak;
And thai in hy tuk all the bak.
And thai, that folowit thaim, has slane
Sum off thaim that thai haf our tane.'—*Barbour*, p. 237.

[7] 'Quhen that the king reparyt was,
That gert his men all leve the chas,
The lordis off his cumpany
Blamyt him, as thai durst, gretumly,
That he him put in auentur,
To mete sa styth a knycht, and sture,
In sic poynt as he then wes sene.
For thai [said], weill it mycht haiff bene
Cause off thair tynsaill euirilkan.
The king ansuer has maid thaim nane;
Bot menyt hys handax schaft, sua
Was with the strak brokyn in twa.'—*Barbour*, p. 237.

quishing Lord Clifford's cavalry, many saddles were empty, and around lay a heap of men and horses wounded and dying. The English had drawn back by degrees, and on taking the direct way to their own countrymen, several of the lingerers last in the flight were pursued, and either taken or slain.[8] When the Scots found they were victorious, they leisurely raised their basinets, and wiping the perspiration from their faces, ascertained their loss was very slight, though we can scarcely be induced to believe it amounted only to one man.[9] On Randolph rejoining

---

[8] 'Bath horss and men slane left thai thar;
And held thair way, in full gret hy,
Nocht all to gyddyr bot syndryly.
And thai that war owrtane war slayn,
The lave went till thair ost agayne,
Off thair tynsaill sary and wa.'—*Barbour*, p. 239.

Among the prisoners was Sir Thomas Gray of Heton, to whose son we are indebted for the translation from French rhyme into French prose of the valuable history entitled 'Scalacronica.'— *Raine*, p. 327. A translation into English of several notable things therein was made by the celebrated antiquary John Leland, and printed in his *Collectanea*, vol. ii. pp. 509-79. This was reprinted in the appendix to the whole work issued in 1836 by the Maitland Club, under the editorship of Joseph Stevenson, Esq., a gentleman to whom every lover of northern history is greatly indebted for the several volumes, either in the original or by translation, which have come forth under his own hand.

[9] 'The erle, that had him helpyn sua,
And his als, that were wery,
Hynt off thair bassynettis in hy,
Till awent thaim; for thai war wate,
Thai war all helyt into swate.

. . . . .

Thai fand off all thair cumpany
That thar wes bot a yuman slayne.'—*Barbour*, p. 239.

the army, Robert Bruce, learning of his success in performing such a gallant achievement, gave him and the cavalry most hearty welcome, while the other warriors crowded around, anxious to behold such noble heroes, and awarding them the honour and glory which they so justly deserved.[10]

On the English being thrown back in both these instances, Bruce collected his chief men around him, and again admonished them to take heart—to praise and love the Almighty, for such a prosperous beginning indicated a favourable termination. The success, he observed, already won would operate to the discomfort and dismay of their adversaries, more especially as the troop under Clifford consisted of the most powerful and courageous men in the English army. Good fortune, no doubt, from the sacred cause for which Scotland fought, would attend her gallant sons; and here again he appealed to his adherents, as he did not say this that his own desire for battle might be followed, but he was ready in every respect to do as those around him should recommend for the welfare of themselves and their country, and therefore he wished them to give free expression to their thoughts.[11] On the instant a shout

---

[10] ' And gladsome cher to thaim mad,
For thai sa weile thaim borne had.
Than all pressyt in to gret daynté
The erle off Murreff for to se:
For his hey worschip, and gret valour,
All yarnyt to do him honour.'—*Barbour*, p. 239.

[11] "' And quhethir I say nocht this yow till,
' For that ye suld folow my will
' To fycht; bot in yow all sall be.
' For giff yow thinkis speidfull that we
' Fecht, we sall; and giff ye will,

arose from the listeners near, who declared that if no assault on the part of England took place that evening, they wished the good King to place them in order of battle on the morning of the following day, and that neither trial nor dread of death should move them in any way till they had given freedom to their own land.[12] Bruce was delighted on hearing this expression of patriotic daring, and rejoicing in their valour and hardihood, he observed that since it was their desire, they should array themselves for fight next morning, and, on hearing mass, each man would take his place under the displayed banner of his respective leader.

---

     ' We leve, your liking to fulfil.
     ' I sall consent, on alkyn wiss,
     ' To do, rycht as ye will dywyss "—*Barbour*, p 240
[12] ' And with a woce than gan thai cry;
     ' Gud king, for owtyn mar delay,
     ' To morne alsone as ye se day,
     ' Ordane yow hale for the bataill.
     ' For doute off dede we sall nocht faill :
     ' Na na payn sall refusyt be,
     ' Quhill we haiff maid our countré fre !"
         *Barbour*, pp. 240-1

## CHAPTER VII.

#### PREPARATION FOR BATTLE.

The weary sun hath made a golden set,
And, by the bright track of his fiery car,
Gives signal of a goodly day to-morrow.
                                SHAKESPEARE.

BY way of admonishing his chief men and those near him how the battle should be conducted, and of acquainting them with his own opinion of the crisis at hand, the King continued to say that of one thing especially he would remind them, which was, not to break the array, for no man must go beyond the line of his own comrades, else disaster would ensue.[1] Also, as they respected him, when

---

[1] "And luk ye na wiss brek aray."—*Barbour*, p. 241.

Bruce, from his long experience in war, knew well how essential it was to success that discipline should be strictly observed in those ranks who were placed front to front with the enemy. We learn from Barbour that, three years after the battle of Bannockburn, the King was in Ireland, and having issued orders that none should quit the ranks, the following incident we give in the language of his biographer:—'Two English yeomen having discharged their arrows against Sir Colin Campbell, the King's nephew, he rashly rode off, at full speed, to avenge the insult, forgetful of the strict injunctions which had just been issued. The King, highly offended at this flagrant breach of discipline, immediately followed, and struck his nephew so violently with his truncheon, that he was nearly beaten from his horse. 'Such breach of orders,' said the King, 'might occasion the loss of the whole army.' '—*Kerr*, vol. ii. p. 85.

they came front to front with the foe, each man with his whole heart and might would, he trusted, do the very utmost in his power to overthrow the strength of the English. They would come in full career on horseback, probably at the gallop, but let them be met by an insurmountable barrier of levelled spears, so that the very last of the troop should feel the opposing shock.[2] He would likewise have his warriors to remember the evil Scotland had endured from the people of England, and what she might still suffer were they not stayed in their hostile intention. As the matter stood, those beside him had three advantages, which he would enumerate. In the first place, the right was on their side, and God would thereby bestow his favour upon them. Secondly, the English approached in full dependence of their own power to capture the Scottish people, and brought hither riches in abundance, so that if victory be on the side of Scotland, the poorest of her sons shall share in the spoil. And thirdly, it was for the lives of the brave men around him, for their children, and for their wives, for the liberty and freedom of their own land, that they go into battle, since the foe had come to destroy them, and would have no mercy upon them were they to suffer defeat in the field.[3] It became them,

---

[2] "On horss thai will arayit rid;
 'And cum on yow in full gret hy.
 'Mete thaim with speris hardely
 'And think than on the mekill ill,
 'That thai and tharis has done ws till,
 'And ar in will yeit for to do,
 'Giff thai haf mycht to cum thar to"
 *Barbour*, p. 241.

[3] "'For we haff thre gret awantagis.
 'The fyrst is, that we haf the rycht,

therefore, to set bravery against wrong, whereby he prayed them to be most alert at the commencement of the struggle, and meet the enemy at the first onset so sternly that all their ranks in the rear might be impressed with dread and dismay.[4] Honour, fame, and wealth, freedom and happiness, would be inherited by them all, did they acquit themselves like men. In order that they might not live in thraldom, they had come with him to do battle for liberty. Greater suffering could not befall them than to be defeated, for, as the English murdered his brother Neill, so would

---

' And for the rycht ay God will fycht.
' The tothyr is, that thai cummyn ar,
' For lyppynnyng off thair gret powar,
' To sek ws in our awne land;
' And has broucht her, rycht till our hand,
' Ryches in to sa gret quantité,
' That the powrest of yow sall be
' Bath rych, and mychty thar with all,
' Giff that we wyne, as weill may fall.
' The thrid is, that we for our lyvis,
' And for our childre, and for our wywis,
' And for our fredome, and for our land,
' Ar strenyeit in to bataill for to stand.
' And thai, for thair mycht ancrly,
' And for thai lat of ws heychtly,
' And for thai wald distroy ws all,
' Maiss thaim to fycht."—*Barbour*, pp. 241-2.

[4] " Quharfor I yow requer, and pray,
' That with all your mycht, that ye may,
' Ye press yow at the begynnyng,
' But cowardyss or abaysing,
' To mete thaim at thair fyrst assemble
' Sa stoutly that the henmaist trymble."
*Barbour*, p. 242.

they also put those around him and himself to death.[5] Of this, however, he had no fear, for by the prowess and strength of these his adherents, they would, through help from above, overcome the foe, especially as the place they were in afforded ample scope for their own movement, but gave insufficient room to their opponents, while it was so defended by nature that those with him could not possibly be outflanked or surrounded. He also beseeched them that none, through desire of gain, would attempt either to plunder or take prisoners till the field was clear of enemies, and then the whole spoil would be their own.[6] Were this

---

[5] "'And I warne yow weill off a thing;
'That mar myscheff may fall ws nane,
'Than in thair handys to be tane:
'For thai suld sla ws, I wate weill,
'Rycht as thai did my brothyr Nele."
Barbour, p. 243.

When the castle of Kildrummie surrendered in 1306, 'Nigel, the brother of Bruce, a youth of singular comeliness, was among the captives. He was tried by a special commission at Berwick, condemned, hanged, and afterwards beheaded.'—*Hailes*, vol. ii. pp. 13-4.

[6] "'For strenth off this place, as ye se,
'Sall let* us enweronyt to be.
'And I pray yow als specially,
'Bath mar and les commonaly,
'That nane of yow for gredynes
'Haff ey to tak of thair ryches;
'Na prisoneris for to ta;
'Quhill ye se thaim contraryit sa,
'That the feld anerly yowris be.
'And than, at your liking, may ye
'Tak all the riches that thar is."
Barbour, pp. 243-4.

* *Let*—prevent.

done, they would undoubtedly be honoured with victory.[7] Further, with judicious foresight, he announced that whoever fell in the struggle, his heirs, however young, should instantly succeed to the inheritance, free of any ward or relief.[8] And now, he continued, let all prepare and be ready for battle, and may God assist and enable us so to meet our enemy that we may come off victorious from the field ![9]

---

[7] " Giff ye will wyrk apon this wiss,
 'Ye sall haiff wictour sekyrly.''—*Barbour*, p. 244.

[8] " And Ik hycht her in leauté ;
 ' Giff ony deys in this bataille,
 ' His ayr, but ward, releff, or taile,
 ' On the fyrst day sall weld ;
 ' All be he neuir sa young off eild.''
*Barbour*, p. 244.

The same concession was made by James the Fourth at Twizelhaugh, 23d August 1513, to the chief men of his army, previous to the battle of Flodden.—*Scots Acts*, p. 98.

[9] " Now makys yow redy for to fycht.
 ' God help ws, that is maist of mycht !
 ' I rede, armyt all nycht that we be,
 ' Purwayit in bataill sua, that we
 ' To mete our fayis ay be boune.''
*Barbour*, p. 244.

The author has not marked the speech of Bruce with points, as if the King had actually uttered it, for though Barbour ascribes it to him, the poetical churchman may have partly embellished it from his own imagination. Still it well merits attention, for human feeling and passion are the same all over the world. In 'The Persians' of *Æschylus*, the solemn outburst of patriotism rising from the Greeks, as they moved to the sea-fight of Salamis, may well form a text to the admonition of the Scottish King :—

" Sons of the Greeks, advance !
 ' Your country free, your children, and your wives,

A general and enthusiastic cry arose that every arrangement should be carried out as the King had proposed, and while the English seemed to halt till the arrears of their army came forward, the Scots made preparation to rest, retiring to a wood in the rear, which afforded some slight shelter from the dews of night, keeping watch, at the same time, that no sudden movement of the foe should take place without due notice of their approach.

The church, on this occasion, lent its aid to work on the superstitious impressions of the King and the army. Bruce, it appears, was in possession of the miraculous arm of St. Fillan, and the relic being enclosed in a silver case, the King had it generally borne at the head of his army. But his chaplain, foreseeing the danger to which the Scots were exposed, and having slight faith in their prowess against the English, had left the arm behind him in a secure place, and brought the empty casket, which was placed in the tent of the King. During the night, when the monarch was engaged in his devotions to God and St. Fillan, the lid of the case, it is written, opened of itself, and suddenly closing, the priest exclaimed that a marvel had been wrought, for the arm was there, and that this betokened success to the Scots![10] Bruce, like a wise

---

'The temples of your fathers' gods,
'Your fathers' sepulchres—
'All—all are now at stake.''

[10] 'But King Robert all the night before the battell tooke litle rest, having great care in his mind for the suertie of his armie, one while revolving in his consideration this chance, and another while that; yea, and sometimes he fell to devout contemplation, making his praier to God and Saint Phillane, whose arme, as it was set and inclosed in a silver case, he supposed had beene the same time within his tent, trusting the better fortune to follow

man, turned this to the best account, and there can be no doubt that he spent the night in anxious thought, wrestling, as it were, to provide in every way for the impending crisis of his fortune on the morrow. In this feeling, and in dependence on the Most High, we may be assured he was cordially seconded by the whole army.

Hollinshed, drawing his statement from Boece, says that on the day before the battle, when two knights of Brabant, in the English army, heard many reproachful words spoken of King Robert Bruce, they, disliking such expressions, had the hardihood to observe they wished victory might fall to him. On this being reported to King Edward, he caused them by trumpet to be sent in derision to the Scottish army, that they might, according to their remarks, render aid to the enemy. He then caused proclamation to be made that whoever brought the heads of these men to him should, by way of recompense, receive one hundred marks.[11]

During the night, it is said, a Scotsman, Alexander Seton by name, who was in the English army, deserted, and arriving at the Scottish camp, communicated the in-

---

by presence thereof. In the meane time, as he was thus making his praiers, the case suddenlie opened, and clapped to againe. The King's chapleine being present, astonied therewith, went to where the case stood, and finding the arme within it, he cried to the King and other that were present, how there was a great miracle wrought, confessing that he brought the emptie case to the field, and left the arme at home, least that relike should have beene lost in the field, if any thing chanced to the armie otherwise than well.'
—*Hollinshed*, pp. 217-8. 'Macgregor, who furnished the relic of St. Fillan, which had been preserved on his lands of Strathfillan, is said to have fought bravely at Bannockburn.'—*Nimmo*, vol. i. p. 209. [11] *Hollinshed*, p. 220.

telligence to Bruce that were he to join battle early next morning he would easily overcome the English.[12] The King, however, depended on the security of his position and other circumstances too much to run the hazard of an unorganised attack, and the result proved eminently successful.

But when the English saw and heard how Clifford with his cavalry had been defeated and beaten off by Randolph, how the van under the Earls of Gloucester and Hereford had been driven back, how Robert Bruce had slain Henry de Bohun, a stalwart knight, with his own hand, and how the Scottish army seemed determined for battle, they were much discomforted, observing among themselves that their chief men led them to the conflict, but that they were to fight in an unjust cause, and that God loved what was right, and would accordingly punish those who were in the wrong.[13] The chief earls and barons of England, on hearing this, caused heralds to proclaim throughout the host that the fighting men were not to be dismayed in any way, but to take courage and behold their great numbers and their prowess, which no enemy was able to withstand.[14]

---

[12] *Leland's Coll.*, vol. ii. pp. 546-7.

[13] ' The Inglis [men] sic abasing
Tuk, and sik dreid of that tithing,
That in fyve hundre placis and ma
Men mycht se samyn routand ga,
Sayand ; ' Our lordis, for thair mycht,
' Will allgate fecht agane the rycht
' Bot quha sa werrayis wrangwysly,
' Thai fend God all to gretumly.
' And thaim may happen to mysfall.
' And swa may tid that her we sall."—*Barbour*, p. 245

[14] ' And quhen thair lordys had persawing
Off discomfort, and rownnyng,

All were also admonished to fight stoutly, thereby maintaining their own honour, and that of England.

King Edward having, with the advice of his nobles, resolved not to commence battle till next morning, the numerous divisions of his troops prepared to rest for the night, several detachments encamping on the spots they occupied, and others descending to the low and fertile grounds, which spread like a carse,[15] and at that time may

---

> That thai held samyn twa and twa;
> Throw out the ost than gart thai ga
> Heraldis, to mak a crye,
> That nane discomfort[yt] suld be;
> \*     \*     \*     \*
> Bot giff the Scottis fley thair way,
> Sall all amendyt be perfay.
> Tharfor thai monest thaim to be
> Off gret worschip, and of bounté;
> And stoutly in the bataill stand,
> And tak amendis at thair hand.'—*Barbour*, pp. 245-6.

[15] Barbour states how the English harboured down in the carse. The term is now applied to the broad level ground bordering on the Forth, which is upwards of a mile to the north-east from the locality where the army was stationed. That chronicler, authentic in almost every instance as we believe him to be, may make an occasional slip, and it is only our duty to notice the following, which crops out at this stage of the narrative. He says:—

> 'And, for in the Kers pulis war,
> Howssis thai brak, and thak bar
> To mak briggis, quhar thai mycht pass.
> And sum sayis yeit, the folk that was
> In the castell, quhen nycht gan fall,
> For that thai knew the myscheiff all,
> Thai went full ner all that thai war,
> And duris and wyndowys with thaim bar;
> Swa that thai had, befor the day,

have been named so, all along the side of Bannockburn. As has been stated, it was now the vigil of St. John, and many in the camp, well knowing the solemn position in which they were placed, must have prepared themselves consistently to take their fortune whatever might befall. Others again, and probably the more numerous class, wearied with the march, and taking advantage of the time, spent the night in drunkenness, revelry, and disorder.[16] In all communities there are reckless men who, though danger be imminent, are bent on enjoying the present hour, and, accordingly, when opportunity occurs, give themselves up to every bodily indulgence. The English camp, therefore, must have presented a very different aspect from that in which the Scots were assembled, waiting to work out their own liberty, and the independence of their father land.

---

> Briggyt the pulis ; swa that thai
> War passyt our ilkane all hale,
> Arayit in till thair apparaill.'—*Barbour*, pp. 246-7.

It seems to us impossible that this could be done, for the watch set by the Scots must effectually have prevented any interference of that kind.

[16] *Moore*, p. 594. See also Baston's verses in *Fordun*, vol. ii. pp. 251-5.

## CHAPTER VIII.

#### THE ARMIES CONFRONT EACH OTHER.

> Yonder my valiant sons and feirs
>  Our raging reivers wait
> On the unconquer'd Scottish sward
>  To try with us their fate.
> Make orisons to Him that saved
>  Our sauls upon the rude;
> Syne bravely shaw your veins are fill'd
>  With Caledonian blude!
> 
> HARDYKNUTE, Stanzas xx.-xxi.
>
> Now's the day, and now's the hour,
> See the front o' battle lour,'
> See approach proud Edward's power,
>  Edward! chains and slavery!
>  \*    \*    \*    \*
> Wha for *Scotland's* king and law
> *Freedom's* sword will freely draw?
> Freeman stand, or Freeman fa',
>  Caledonian! on wi' me!—BURNS.

ON the morning of Monday, the 24th June 1314, Bruce observed the English army in the exact position he wished it to be, consequently he drew up his squadrons on the ground he had selected for battle. Having signified his wish that the brave warriors before him should receive the sacrament, Maurice, Abbot of Inchaffray, in Strathearn, Perthshire, who accompanied the King, performed mass on an eminence in front of the Scottish army, desiring all to confess their sins and supplicate God on behalf of their country.[1] The troops then partook of breakfast, which partly consisted of bread and wine,[2] and then deliberately made themselves ready for the struggle. Next, they took their places under their respective banners, which we may suppose streamed brightly in the morning breeze. Bruce, in the company of his leading men, proceeded, according to the custom before battle at that time, to confer knighthood on Walter Steward, James Douglas, and other gallant warriors, who were deserving of such honour, each being promoted according to his degree.[3] Then each division went forward and occupied the place assigned to it, filling up the line of battle as arranged by the King, and the whole extended from the hollow north of Halbert's Bog, upwards to the south-west on the high ground, near the bend of the Bannock above Park Mill.[4] Retaining pos-

---

[1] 'On the morow, he gaderit al his army to messe to ressave the body of God, to mak thaim have the more curage aganis thair ennimes. In this army wes ane devoit man, named Maritius, Abbot of Inchechaffray, quhilk said messe on ane hie mote, and ministerit the Eucharist to the King and his nobillis; and causit his preistis to mak ministratioun thairof to the residew of the army.'—*Bellenden*, vol. ii. p. 391.

[2] 'Bruce refreshed his troops with bread and wine.'—*Turner*, vol. ii. p. 141.

[3] 'The king maid Walter Stewart knycht;
And James of Dowglas, that wes wycht;
And othyr als of gret bounté
He maid, ilk ane in thar degree.'—*Barbour*, p. 248.

[4] In the large map completed by the Board of Ordnance, the site of the battle is marked close to the south-east side of the road between Coxet Hill and Graystale. The author is not a military man, but from a most careful inspection of the battlefield, taking into account all the circumstances connected with it, he is of opinion

session of this place, while the thoroughfares at Milton and below Brock's Brae were rendered impassable, the Scots could not be outflanked, and hence the English must of necessity be compelled to meet them here in battle. We know not where the trees grew that were near or among the various lines of troops, but portions of wood arose over the whole neighbourhood. Nor do we believe that the entire army was collected together in these several divisions. They might be completed, so far as numbers could be made up, but considerable detachments were doubtless stationed above Milton, or near the Bore-stone, on Coxet Hill, and beyond the extremity of the right wing, at a short distance from Graystale. These were to watch the progress of the contest, and in case any party quitted the main body of the foe and made an advance, the said Scots were to meet and repel them, or at least to convey intimation of the circumstance to the King.

It has been already stated that, according to the direction of Bruce, the Scottish army was to be separated into four divisions, and how the charge of the right wing devolved upon Edward Bruce. The van at first was intended to be led by Randolph, but Bruce, on surveying the ground, would seem to have altered his original plan, for the highest part of the front lines was where his brother was placed, and this point, he well knew, would be first assailed by the enemy. Accordingly, the body of above

---

that the front line of battle, presented at first by the Scots to the enemy, must have been nearly two hundred yards farther to the south. This gave Robert Bruce, from the highest point of the rise directly north of Park Mill, a full view of the whole field, and any impartial man must perceive how necessary this was to the King in regulating every impending movement of his forces.

seven thousand warriors, under Sir Edward Bruce, came to form the van of the Scots, for they were before the others, who were stationed somewhat behind, on lower ground, and their heroic leader had the angle of the stream already mentioned, hid far down among trees, on his right hand. Next him, on his left, but a little to the rear, with a space between the divisions, so narrow as not to allow a passage for the English horse, was Randolph, Earl of Moray, leading a like number of men; and still farther to the north-east, slightly to the rear, also on the lower ground, and near to the head of Halbert's Bog, stood Sir Walter Steward and Sir James Douglas, completing with their spearmen, equal in number to the others, the whole front lines of battle.[5] Taking into account the spaces which separated these divisions, each section would average about fourteen men deep, a force that, judiciously guided, would, if they fought well, accomplish much on a stricken field. Again, on the highest ground beside, or rather behind, Sir Edward Bruce and Randolph, with the fourth division in reserve, the King was stationed on horseback, regulating the whole, and watching attentively from his lofty position every movement, both of his own troops and those of the enemy. Apart from these four bodies of warriors were the five hundred cavalry, who had overcome Clifford, led by Sir Robert Keith, hereditary Marshal of Scotland. Moreover, a considerable band of archers, of whom we are unable to

---

[5] These divisions, be it remembered, were drawn up, as we gather from Barbour, somewhat obliquely, the rear corner to the left of that led by Sir Edward Bruce approaching the front corner to the right of the men under Randolph, and the left rear of his warriors nearing the right front of those headed by the Steward and Douglas.

state the number, were placed probably near the openings of the several divisions, but, on account of the rise of the ground, somewhat near to that of Sir Edward Bruce. At this instant both armies must have presented a stirring and most magnificent sight. Before the King were his own devoted subjects, ready to offer up their lives for the freedom of Scotland; and from the stream of Bannock, mile beyond mile, south-east to the hill of Plean, shaded occasionally by patches of the forest, but covering the whole side of the declivity which sloped down towards the brook, one enormous crowd appeared of men, horses, and carriages.[6] The latter were stationed more in the distance, but in front and behind, up to and beyond Foot o' Green, were banners, flags, and pennons, of every colour, waving beyond each other in the breeze, while armour, shields, helmets, morions, and weapons, glanced and sparkled above the bearers far and wide.[7] Earls, knights, and bannerets on horseback, gorgeously decorated in their sur-

[6] ' Thai went all furth in gud aray;
And tuk the plane full apertly.
Mony gud man, wicht and hardy,
That war fulfillyt of gret bounté,
In till thai rowtis men mycht se.
The Inglis men, on othyr party,
That as angelis schane brychtly,
War nocht arayit on sic maner:
For all thair bataillis samyn wer
In a schilthrum.'—*Barbour*, p. 248.

[7] ' Quhar mony a schynand scheld,
And mony a burnyst brycht armur,
And mony a man off gret walur,
Mycht in that gret schiltrum be sene;
And mony a brycht baner and schene.'
*Barbour*, p. 249.

coats of various bright hues, seemed innumerable, while squires, cavalry, and infantry, comprising spearmen and archers, densely mingled together, filled up every available space of ground. Their immense numbers scarcely allowed of any opening between them, and we may readily conclude that no exhibition of martial pomp and grandeur to an equal extent was ever witnessed in this land. Fancy delights to contemplate the gorgeous display, and we may conceive how it thrilled the heart of Bruce, and awakened feelings of awe and sublimity in the bosoms, not only of his noble adherents, but of many a brave Scottish peasant.[8]

Ere the English moved forward, several of the leading men of mature age, knowing how the greater part of the army, by watching and revelry through the night, had en-

---

[8] Making some allowance for verbosity, the following description of the scene deserves attention :—

'Be this wes said the browdin baneris brycht
Aboue thair heid wes haldin vp on hicht,
Flureist and frie, weill wrocht ouir with gold wyre,
Glitterand as gleid or Phebus flammand fyre;
And staithe standartis streikit in the air,
Wyde witht the wynd waiffand heir and thair,
Of siluer, sabill, and of asur blew,
Depantit ouir with mony sindrie hew,
With rosis, lillie, and with flourdelyce,
And mony pynsall precious wes of pryce,
Agane the schyning of the sone tha schew,
Palit with purpure and with asur blew.
Thair basnetis bricht with mony bureall stone,
Agane the schyning of the sone tha schone ;
Baith helme and habrik wes of hevenlie hew,
Lyke schynand siluer ouir the schaw that schew,
With breist [plait], brasar, and with birneis bricht,
Lyke ony lanterne lemit all of licht.'

*Stewart*, vol. iii pp. 231-2.

joyed little or no sleep, endeavoured to prevail with the King to defer the conflict till the following day, but the younger chiefs derided such counsel, and the prudence of the former was set aside. The Earl of Gloucester advocated delay, and the King foolishly called him a traitor for his discretion. The taunt was indignantly repelled by the remark that before the day was over proof would be given he was neither traitor nor coward.[9] It was some time ere the arrangements for commencing the attack were completed, and thus the leaders lingered that they might receive orders to advance.

Meantime King Edward was accompanied by Aymer de Valence, Earl of Pembroke, on one side of his bridle, and Sir Giles de Argentine, one of the bravest knights in Europe, at the other, also bishops and ecclesiastics who kept near to him, together with five hundred armed horsemen as his body-guard. It would appear he was stationed somewhere in the neighbourhood of Chartershall Mains, and when gazing northward, on observing the Scottish army drawn up in hostile array, all on foot, he was somewhat amazed at the sight. Looking at the enormous numbers of his own forces, he considered they must be invincible in battle, wherever and whenever it took place; nor did it even enter his mind either to lead them on under superior generalship, or cause them to meet the enemy upon suitable ground, in order to come off victorious. Believing, therefore, that Bruce's army would not dare to oppose him, he inquired of Sir Ingram de Umfreville, who knew them well, 'If yonder Scots would presume to fight?' 'Yea, surely, sire,' said the knight, 'and it is the most fearful sight I ever

---

[9] *Mon. Malm.* p. 149.   *Turner*, vol. ii. pp. 140-1.

beheld, when they are resolved to do battle against the whole force of England. Truly I know the people, and if your Majesty would please to follow my advice, I can devise how they may easily be overcome. Let us withdraw the army and retreat, as if for fear, beyond our baggage and pavilions, on our way to England, and the desire of spoil shall so work upon them that no captain may keep them together, and thus, when their ranks are broken, we shall secure an easy victory.'[10] 'I will not assent to this,'

---

[10] ' And quhen the king off Ingland
Swa the Scottis saw tak on hand,
Takand the hard feyld sa opynly,
And apon fute, he had ferly;
And said, ' Quhat ! will yone Scottis fycht ?'
' Ya sekyrly !' said a knycht,
Schyr Ingrame the Wmfrawill hat he ,
And said, ' Forsuth now, Schyr, I se,
' It is the mast ferlyfull sycht
' That euyre I saw, quhen for to fycht
' The Scottis men has tane on hand,
' Agayne the mycht of Ingland,
' In plane hard feild, to giff bataile
' Bot, and ye will trow my consaill,
' Ye sall discomfyt thaim lychtly.
' Withdrawys yow hyne sodandly,
' With bataillis, and with penownys,
' Quhill that we pass our pailyownyis ;
' And ye sall se alsone that thai,
' Magre thair lordys, sall brek aray,
' And scaile thaim our harnays to ta.
' And, quhen we se thaim scalit sua,
' Prik we than on thaim hardely,
' And we sall haf thaim wele lychtly.
' For than sall nane be knyt to fycht,
' That may withstand your mekill mycht.'—
' I will nocht,' said the king, ' perfay,

said the King, 'nor will I turn from doing battle with such a low, despicable concourse of people.' By this time the Abbot of Inchaffray, who had previously celebrated mass, now advanced, walking bare-footed along the front of the Scottish lines as they stood prepared for the onset, and carrying a cross wherein a crucifix was suspended, he raised it as a banner,[11] and admonished his countrymen in most earnest and appropriate words to perform their duty nobly in so righteous and glorious a cause.[12] When he had done this, the whole army knelt down, and confessing their shortcomings, put up a brief but fervent prayer that the Almighty would remember them in mercy, and crown their efforts with success.[13]

---

'Do sa: for thar sall na man say,
'That I sall eschew the bataill,
'Na withdraw me for sic rangaile."
*Barbour*, pp. 249-50.

[11] 'Maritius, the abbot forsaid, tuke the croce, in quhilk the crucifix wes hinging, and ereckit it afore the army in mauer of ane baner.'—*Bellenden*, vol. ii. p. 392.

[12] 'The abbat of Inchchaffraie, aforesaid, came forth before the battels, with the crucifix in his hands, bearing it aloft like a standard, admonishing them valiantlie to take in hand the defense of their countrie and the libertie of their posteritie; for, saith he, you must not euerie man fight as it were for his own privat defense, his own house and children, but euerie man for all men, and all men for euerie man, must fight for the libertie, life, patrimonie, children, and wiues of all the realme; for such and so great is the dignitie of our countrie as they which deface or spoile are to be punished with perpetuall fier, and they which doo preserve it are to be recompensed with an eternal crowne of glorie.'—*Hollinshed*, p. 219.

[13] 'Quhen this wes said, that er said I,
The Scottis men comounaly

When all the divisions of the Scots thus knelt down, King Edward, who beheld them, believed they were supplicating for pardon, and turning again to Umfreville, observed, 'These people dare not encounter us in the field—see they all kneel to us for mercy!' 'They do seek for mercy, my liege,' said the knight, 'but not from your Majesty. They implore Heaven for pardon and for help in the struggle, and believe me, sire, these men will either win or die where they stand, nor will they fly for all the power England can bring against them.' 'Be it so, then,' said the King, and almost immediately after the trumpets sounded the onset of battle [14]

> Knelyt all doune, to God to pray
> And a schort prayer thar maid thai
> To God, to help thaim in that fycht.'
> 
> *Barbour*, p 250.

'And when ye are come near unto the battle, then the Priest shall come forth and speak unto the people

'And shall say unto them, Hear, O Israel, ye are come this day unto battle against your enemies

'Let not your hearts faint, neither fear nor be amazed, nor adread of them.

'For the Lord your God goeth with you to fight for you against your enemies, and to save you.'—*Deuteronomy*, chap. xx, verses 2-4.

An additional example is hereby shown of what may be performed by men who solemnly put their trust in and implore the Most High for help in the hour of need. Cromwell's forces under such influence, and by his able guidance, were almost invariably led on to victory.

[14] 'And quhen the Inglis king had sycht
Oft thaim kneland, he said in hy,
'Yone folk knel to ask mercy.'
Schyr Ingrahame said, 'Ye say suth now.
'Thai ask mercy, bot nane at yow.
'For thair trespas to God thai cry

'I tell you a thing sekyrly;
'That yone men will all wyn or de:
'For doute of dede thai sall nocht fle.'—
'Now be it sa than;' said the king.
And than, but\* langer delaying,
Thai gert trump till the assemblé.
On athir sid men mycht than se
Mony a wycht man, and worthi,
Redy to do chewalry.'—*Barbour*, p. 250.

---

\* *But*—without.

## CHAPTER IX.

#### THE BATTLE COMMENCES.

Now on each side the leaders
    Gave signal for the charge;
And on each side the footmen
    Strode on with lance and targe;
And on each side the horsemen
    Struck their deep spurs in gore;
And front to front the armies
    Met with a mighty roar.
\*      \*      \*      \*
And louder still and louder
    Rose from the darkened field
The braying of the war horns,
    The clang of sword and shield,
The rush of squadrons sweeping
    Like whirlwinds o'er the plain,
The shouting of the slayers,
    And screeching of the slain.—MACAULAY.

SCOTIA's bard has given us an animated 'Address of Bruce to his Army' in a measure to suit the old stirring tune, which tradition sanctions as the 'March' of the patriot on the present occasion. Rude war-pipes or horns might give forth awakening notes to thrill the bosoms of the Scots, but that the ranks moved forward we consider very doubtful. It is more probable that, like the rocks of their own sea-girt land, they firmly awaited the approach of their foes only to dash them back like ocean waves broken in a boisterous storm. The van of the English, consisting of armed men and horse under the Earls of Gloucester and Hereford, flanked on the left by the archers, held on up the slope, direct to the foremost Scottish division, headed by Sir Edward Bruce;[1] and it seems probable they charged at the quick trot or gallop, with great fury.[2] Owing, however, to a dispute between the leaders, and to the consequent irregularity of the movement, the English being partly broken, made little or no impression on the Scottish lines, though several on both sides were slain.[3] The cause why the division of Sir

---

[1] Moore blames the English cavalry for beginning the struggle while the sun was shining on their gilt shields and burnished helms, instead of waiting till noon. See also *Meyrick*, vol. i. p. 206, and *Turner*, vol. ii. p. 142. This is clearly a mistake, for the sun rose to the right of the English in the morning, he shone on their backs towards noon, and was descending on their left to the west when the Scots gained the victory.

[2] 'Thus war thai boune on athir sid.
And Inglis men, with mekill prid,
That war in till thair awaward,
To the bataill that Schyr Eduuard
Gowernyt and led, held straucht thair way.
The horss with spuris hardnyt thai;
And prikyt apon thaim sturdely;
And thai met thaim rycht hardely;
Swa that, at thair assemblé thar,
Sic a fruschyng of speris war,
That fer away men mycht it her.'—*Barbour*, pp. 250-1.

[3] 'The English van, led by Gloucester and Hereford, now spurred forward their horses, and at full gallop charged the right wing of the Scots, commanded by Edward Bruce; but a dispute as to precedence caused the charge, though rapid, to be broken and irregular. Gloucester, who had been irritated the day before by some galling remarks of the King, insisted on leading the van, a post which of right belonged to Hereford as Constable of Eng-

Edward Bruce was first encountered might be that this body occupied, as has been stated, the highest ground on the battle-field, that it was in advance of the other divisions, and that the attack could be made more effectual on this point from the shield borne on the left arm of the Scottish soldier, leaving the right side more exposed to the sword or spear. All this King Robert seems to have foreseen, and made his arrangements accordingly. Here also we may perceive how the English archers knowingly flanked the left of the van, and thereby obtained the loftiest position, whence their shafts might fly with more deadly aim against the Scots. The shock was tremendous, for the men-at-arms rushed onward as if to break through the serried barrier of spears, probably two or three yards broad;[4] and though some of the Scots were borne to the

---

land. To this Hereford would not agree; and Gloucester, as they disputed, seeing the Scottish right advancing, sprang forward at the head of his own division, and, without being supported by the rest of the van, attacked the enemy, who received them with a shock which caused the meeting of their spears to be heard a great way off, and threw many knights from their saddles whose horses were stabbed and rendered furious by their wounds.'— *Tytler*, vol. i. pp. 270-1.

[4] ' Bruce compacted his men into a thick mass, a bristled hedge, like the Macedonian phalanx, which from its union and solidity was impenetrable.'—*Turner*, vol. ii. p. 140.

' Before the battle of Arbela, Alexander formed his men sixteen deep, and placed in their grasp the *sarissa*, as the Macedonian pike was called, and which was twenty-four feet in length, and when couched for action reached eighteen feet in front of the soldier; so that, as a space of two feet was allowed between the ranks, the spears of the five files behind him projected in front of each front-rank man.'—*Creasy*, vol. i. p. 124; *Grote*, vol. viii. pp. 226, 292-3, 459.

## THE BATTLE COMMENCES. 91

earth, many of their assailants were overthrown.[5] The horses which were pierced plunged wildly, and their riders falling, were either trampled upon by others, or when a slight advance was made, they were struck to death by the Scottish axes. At every onset the crash of broken spears might be heard at a great distance. Still the Scots stood firm as onward came the cavalry without ceasing, while the English archers, who were distant nearly twelve score yards, poured incessantly into the dense masses of the opposing spearmen their showers of arrows, each about three feet long. Some of the English chroniclers say that several of these fell short of their aim, and pierced the undefended backs of their own people.[6] The latter, who were on horseback, would more readily intercept the flight of these shafts when aimed at the Scots, whose front lines were all on foot.

The remaining divisions of the English, who were compressed together as if they formed one column of enormous length and breadth, began partly to deploy on crossing the Bannock, and advancing upwards to the field, threw themselves in succession headlong upon the foe. That body of the Scots under the command of the redoubted Randolph, who were stationed near those already fighting that the latter might not be taken in flank, met the assailants in line, and maintained their ground gallantly, repelling the

---

[5]  \*    \*    'for hardely
Thai dang on othyr with wapnys ser.
Sum of the horss, that stekyt wer,
Ruschyt, and relyt rycht rudlye.' —*Barbour*, p. 251.

[6] 'When they shot right forth they slew fewe of the Scots by reason of their armed breasts, but many of the Englishmen by reason of their naked backs.'—*Moore*, p. 594, quoted by Stowe, p. 217.

horsemen and foot with the same bravery as their fellow-warriors to the right had shown.[7] The encounter was not less fierce than before, for not a foot were the Scots driven back, but they rather advanced, treading over every obstacle in their way.[8] Besides, they adhered strictly to the command of the King, for they kept closely, shoulder to shoulder, in the line of battle. The array was never broken, but amid the dreadful struggle of man opposed to man, inflicting on each other wounds and death, the Scots, as they pressed forward, seemed plunged in a stormy sea covered with men, horses, and weapons of every kind, which were wielded with tremendous energy.[9] Blood

---

[7] 'And quhen the erle of Murref swa
　　Thair waward saw, sa stoutly, ga
　　The way to Schyr Eduuard all straucht,
　　That met thaim with full mekill maucht.
　　He held hys way, with his baner,
　　To the gret rout quhar samyn wer
　　The nyne bataillis, that war sa braid;
　　That sa fele baneris with thaim haid,
　　And of men sa gret quantité,
　　That it war wondre for to se.'—*Barbour*, pp. 250-1.

[8] 'For thair fayis assemblyt fast,
　　That on stedis, with mekill prid,
　　Come prikand, as thai wald our rid
　　The erle and all his cumpany.
　　Bot thai met thaim sa sturdely,
　　That mony of thaim till erd thai bar.
　　For mony a sted wes stekyt thar;
　　And mony gud man fellyt wndre fet.'
　　　　　　　　　　*Barbour*, p. 252.

[9] 'The erle of Murreff, and his men,
　　Sa stoutly thaim contenyt then,
　　That thai wan place, ay mar and mar,
　　On thair fayis; quhethir thai war

flowed in every direction, and the Scots, though opposed to such overwhelming numbers, still bore onward, the English encountering them most fiercely, and doing all in their power to check the course of these intrepid northern warriors.[10]

The massive columns of English, still pressing onward to the right, came at length into battle with the troops under Sir Walter Steward and Sir James Douglas, who kept near to the division of Randolph and still preserved the front of the Scottish lines unbroken.[11] A similar

---

   Ay ten for ane, or may, perfay;
   Swa that it semyt weill that thai
   War tynt amang sa gret menye,
   As thai war plungyt in the se.'—*Barbour*, pp. 252-3.

[10] 'And quhen the Inglis men has sene
   The erle, and all his men, bedene
   Faucht sa stoutly, but effraying,
   Rycht as thai had nane abasing;
   Thaim pressyt thai with all thair mycht.
   And thai, with speris and suerdis brycht,
   And axys that rycht scharply schar,
   Ymyddis the wesag met thaim thar.
   Thar mycht men se a stalwart stour;
   And mony men of gret valour,
   With speris, masis, and knyffis,
   And othyr wapynnys, wyssyllyt thair lyvis:
   Swa that mony fell doune all dede.
   The greyss woux with the blud all reid.'
          *Barbour*, p. 253.

[11] 'Quhen thir twa fyrst bataillis wer
   Assemblyt, as I said yow er,
   The Stewart, Waltre that than was,
   And the gud lord als of Douglas,
   In a bataill, quhen that thai saw
   The erle, for owtyn dred or aw,

onslaught was made by the enemy with still greater vehemence, if possible, in order to break through the opposing Scottish spears, and again the English, both horse and foot, were repelled with the most determined resolution. Steed after steed was thrown down, and knight, squire, and man-at-arms on the side of England fell, yet their places were instantly occupied by the masses behind, and the battle on the whole line became more fierce and terrible. The soil was covered with the dead and the dying, while the struggling combatants waded through coagulated streams of blood,[12] yet no lapse took place in the stern valour everywhere displayed, and the Scots, advancing as they fought, trode over prostrate horse and man as if all opposition was in vain.

> Assembill with his cumpany
> On all that folk sa sturdely,
> For till help him thai held thair way;
> And assemblyt sa hardely
> Besid the erle, a litill by,
> That thair fayis feld thair cummyn wele.
> For with wapynnys stalwart of stele
> Thai dang apon, with all thair mycht.'
> *Barbour*, pp. 253-4.

[12] 'Thar fayis resawyt weile, Ik hycht,
With swerdis, speris, and with mase.
The bataill thar sa feloune was,
And swa rycht gret spilling of blud,
That on the erd the floussis stud.
The Scottis men sa weill thaim bar,
And swa gret slauchter maid thai thar,
And fra sa fele the lyvis rewyt,
That all the feld bludy wes lewyt.
That tyme thar thre bataillis wer,
All syd besid, fechtand weill ner.

## THE BATTLE COMMENCES.

While the armies thus opposed each other in direful conflict, Robert Bruce observed how the shafts from the English bows were telling most fatally on the right wing of his army, especially among his own archers, who were not clothed like the spearmen in defensive armour. For this he was prepared, and giving orders that Sir Robert Keith, Earl Marshal, should lead the troop of five hundred horse under his command against these bowmen, the movement was at once accomplished.[13] Threading their way probably amid the furze and trees that grew on the north-east bank of the Bannock above Park Mill, they outflanked the English cavalry, and, without the slightest opposition, fell on the unarmed men, who were lightly clad and altogether unprotected, for the attention of King Edward and his nobles must at the time have been directed intensely towards the main front of the battle. A brief space

---

Thar mycht men her mony dint,
And wapynnys apon armuris stynt;
And se tumble knychtis, and stedis,
And mony rich and reale wedis
Defoullyt foully wndre fete.'—*Barbour*, p. 254.

[13] 'The Inglis archeris schot sa fast,
That mycht thair schot haff ony last,
It had bene hard to Scottis men.
Bot king Robert, that wele gan ken
That thair archeris war peralouss,
And thair schot rycht hard and grewouss,
Ordanyt, forouth the assemblé,
Hys marschell with a gret menye,
Fyve hundre armyt in to stele,
That on lycht horss war horsyt welle,
For to pryk amang the archeris;
And swa assaile thaim with thair speris,
That thai na layser haiff to schute.'—*Barbour*, p. 255.

elapsed ere Keith Marshal accomplished his mission, but ultimately the English archers were totally defeated.[14] Many were borne to the ground or killed, while those who fled were almost unable, from the pressure, to obtain room among the English troops, hence, during the latter part of the day, they never rallied to afford any especial assistance to their countrymen.[15] Meanwhile, the Scottish archers, though not very expert with the bow, being armed with swords, knives, and battle-axes, now that the shower of steel from their opponents had ceased, came forward and aimed their shafts with most fatal effect on the enemy.

When Robert Bruce saw Keith Marshal return after dispersing the English archers, and also observing before him his three divisions still making way on the enemy, maintaining their squares in line with each other, and fighting most bravely, he was, apart from the excitement, much gratified, for every movement indicated a prosperous result. Addressing the chief men near him who headed

---

[14] 'In hy apon thaim gan he rid,
And our tuk thaim at a sid,
And ruschyt amang thaim sa rudly,
Stekand thaim sa dispitously,
And in sic fusoun berand doun,
And slayand thaim, for owtyn ransoun,
That thai thaim scalyt euirilkane.
And fra that tyme furth thar wes nane
That assemblyt schot to ma'—*Barbour*, p. 255.

[15] 'And agayne armyt men to fycht
May nakyt men have litill mycht.
Thai scalyt thaim on sic maner,
That sum to thair gret bataill wer
Withdrawyn thaim, in full gret hy.
And sum wai fled all wtrely.'—*Barbour*, p. 256

his own division ere they joined in battle, he cheered them with words of encouragement, desiring they also should acquit themselves most gallantly, so that any opposing force might be unable to withstand their onset. The several oblong squares before him were fighting most fiercely, and had so gallantly encountered the foe, that were the latter pressed something more they would doubtless be overcome. 'Now then,' he is reported to have said to the leaders in his own division, 'let us go forward, and support our fellow-countrymen in their glorious cause, for we trust we shall have assistance from on high to punish these assailants as they deserve.'[16] On this being said they

---

[16] 'And the gud king Robert, that ay
Wes fillyt off full gret bounté,
Saw how that his bataillis thre
Sa hardely assemblyt thar,
And sa weill in the fycht thaim bar ;
And swa fast on thair fayis gan ding,
That him thoucht name had abaysing ;
And how the archeris war scalyt then ;
He was all blyth : and till his men
He said ; 'Lordingis, now luk that ye
' Worthy, and off gud cowyn be,
' At thys assemblé, and hardy.
' And assembill sa sturdely,
' That na thing may befor yow stand.
' Our men ar sa freschly fechtand,
' That thai thair fayis has grathyt sua,
' That be thai pressyt, Ik wndreta,
' A litill fastyr, ye sall se
' That thai discumfyt sone sall be.''
*Barbour*, pp. 256-7.

ANOTHER VERSION.
'' Our kin, and our friends . . .
' Despiteously they hang'd and drawn,

advanced chiefly to the right, filling up the weakest portions of the lines, and taking their place where the battle was most fiercely disputed.[17]

---

'And would destroy us if they might;
'But I trow God, through his foresight,
'This day has granted us his grace
'To wreck us on them in this place."
                                    Barbour, B. L. p. 266.

[17] 'Quhen this wes said, thai held thair way;
And on ane feld assemblyt thai
Sa stoutly, that at thair cummyng
Thair fayis war ruschyt a gret thing.'—*Barbour*, p 257.

'It would seem from some expressions in Barbour that the King of Scots brought up the reserve to the right of his army This shows that there had been a great slaughter of the Scots, by which, in that circumscribed ground, there was place left for the reserve to fall into the line.'—*Hailes*, vol ii p. 47

This is every way probable, for Sir Edward Bruce not only withstood the first onset of the English, but sustained it to the last, and being on the highest ground, the strength of the enemy, we may be certain, was chiefly directed to this quarter, which seems to have been all foreseen, and provided for by Bruce

## CHAPTER X.

### BATTLE CONTINUED.

O God, thy arm was here,
And not to us, but to thy arm alone
Ascribe we all!—SHAKESPEARE.

THE whole martial forces of Scotland, except the slight detachments near them in reserve, were now engaged in the fight, so that the ground, from the high banks of the Bannock, north of Park Mill, to the head of Halbert's Bog, and down southward to the Bannock again, was crowded with fighting men, while, in the opposing lines of conflict, each was struggling between life and death for victory. Again and again did the mailed chivalry of England, in heavy masses, attempt to break through the opposing barrier of pointed steel, and as often did they fail, nor could they possibly draw back, for those behind, closely wedged together, would allow of no retreating, and, thus environed on each side, they fell pierced with wounds.[1] Horses sprang away with empty saddles, adding

---

[1] 'Thai faucht, as thai war in a rage.
For quhen the Scottis archery
Saw thair fayis sa sturdely
Stand in to bataill thaim agayn ;
With all thair mycht, and all thair mayn,
Thai layid on, as men out of wit.
And quhar thai, with full strak, mycht hyt,
Thar mycht na armur stynt thair strak.
Thai to fruchyt that thai mycht our tak :

to the general tumult and dismay, while others rolled over with men upon them in mailed armour, who, being unable to rise, were trodden to the earth in helpless confusion. All this time the Scottish archers, winging their shafts where they fell most effectually, performed gallant service; nor did they constantly use the bow, for as occasion served they seized their axes, and so handled them that neither helm nor habergeon could ward off the stroke. It was a fearful struggle, for the whole Scottish front, moving still onward, forced their way, as our national poet says, 'red-wat shod' over every obstacle of men and horses, dead or dying. Nor did the opposite lines of the English seem to slacken in any degree, for everywhere they appeared in countless numbers, taking the place, whenever it occurred, of those who fell, and endeavouring, with determined energy, to break the overwhelming rush of spears, that a gap might be made whereby the cavalry might enter and bear to earth the undaunted Scots.[2] The latter truly

> And with axys sic duschys gave,
> That thai helmys and hedis clave.
> And thar fayis rycht hardely
> Met thaim, and dang on thaim douchtely,
> With wapnys that war styth of stele.'
> *Barbour*, p. 257-8.

[2] 'Thar wes the bataill strekyt wele.
Sa gret dyn thar wes of dyntis,
As wapnys apon armur styntis;
And off speris sa gret bresting;
And sic thrang, and sic thrysting;
Sic gyrnyng, granyng; and sa gret
A noyis, as thai gan othyr beit;
And ensenyeys on ilka sid;
Gewand, and takand, woundis wid;
That it wes hydwyss for to her.

could not maintain their progress unscathed, for many a steady spearman fell, yielding up his breath in stern defence of the liberties of his native land.

Barbour himself soars into the region of poetry on describing the scene, appealing to the great Ruler of the universe, while he writes how Sir Edward Bruce and his gallant warriors acquitted themselves in the fight so nobly that their shock of spears was tremendous, and that the Scots maintained themselves in such a compact body that whoever fell before them never had the power to rise again. Many gallant feats were performed, and many a brave man killed, for the field was red with gore, while surcoats, clothing, and various appendages to garments of brilliant appearance were so stained with soil and blood they could not be known.[3] In the same way our venerable

---

All thair four battailis with that wer
Fechtand in a frount halyly.'—*Barbour*, p. 258.

[3] 'A mychty God! how douchtely
Schyr Edunard the Bruce, and his men,
Amang thair fayis contenyt thaim then!
Fechtand in sa gud covyn,
Sa hardy, worthy, and sa fyne,
That thar waward ruschyt was;

\*  \*  \*  \*

Quha hapnyt in to that fycht to fall,
I trow agane he suld nocht ryss.
Thar mycht men se, on mony wyss,
Hardimentis eschewyt douchtely;
And mony, that wycht war and hardy,
Sone liand wndre fete all dede;
Quhar all the feld off blud wes rede.
Armys, and quhytyss, that thai bar,
With blud war sa defoulyt thar,
That thai mycht nocht descroyit be.'
*Barbour*, pp. 258-9.

chronicler delineates with a skilful hand how the Steward and Douglas, with their power, so pressed the enemy that whoever witnessed it might well say these heroes were worthy of all honour, while many a splendid horse plunged back amid the throng without its rider.[4] Then he alludes to Randolph, telling how he and his devoted soldiers made their way wherever they came, repelling at every step the mailed, courageous, and high-minded chivalry of England.[5] Here and there also, between the divisions of spearmen, the archers plied their bows so incessantly during the desperate struggle of both man and horse, who were only a few yards from them, that almost every arrow flew to its aim, and every axe dealt an irresistible blow. Moreover, the whole front of the Scots, obedient to the strict injunc-

---

[4] 'A mychty God! quha than mycht se
That Stewart, Waltre, and his rout,
And the gud Douglas, that wes sa stout,
Fechtand in to that stalwart stour,
He suld say that till all honour
Thai war worthi, that, in that fycht,
Sa fast pressyt thair fayis mycht,
That thaim ruschyt quhar thai yeid
Thar men mycht se mony a steid
Fleand on stray, that lord had nane.'
                                            *Barbour*, p 259

[5] 'A Lord! quha then gud tent had tane
Till the gud erle of Murreff,
And his, that sa gret rowtis geff,
And faucht sa fast in that battaill,
Tholand sic paynys and trawaill,
That thai and tharis maid sic debat,
That quhar thai come thai maid thaim gat'
                                            *Barbour*, p 259.

tion of the king, was maintained in regular line, for no opening could be made among them, and the English were either slain or driven backward, surely, though at times slowly, yet ever retreating.[6]

This desperate fighting continued for a considerable time, while Robert Bruce observed that assistance was promptly rendered wherever it was required. Accordingly, the English, finding it impossible to make way against the enemy, were amazed, and at length they hesitated to renew the heavy and repeated charges they made at first to break through or circumvent the Scots. This slackness was at once observed by the latter, and among them the cry arose, which soon circulated along the whole lines—'On them, on them!—they fail, they fail!' Every Scotsman thereby felt his heart animated afresh, and in front of the several divisions the assault was sustained with the most desperate energy and enthusiasm. The important event which would echo over Britain for a thousand years was about to be decided, victory on the one side and defeat on the other was imminent, for another hour would in all likelihood determine the problem.

While the battle continued to be struck thus fiercely, the number of camp followers, or gillies, meaning the male servants, and numbering above fifteen thousand, who were sent away from the army, as has been stated, to a hollow north of Graystale, on Gillies Hill, had watched the struggle most attentively from the higher ground, and as they ob-

---

[6] 'For thai, that fechtand with thaim wer,
Set herdement, and strenth, and will,
And hart, and corage als, thar till;
And all thair mayne, and all thair mycht,
To put thaim fully to [the] flycht.'—*Barbour*, p. 260.

served their countrymen not only confronting the English in unbroken lines, but repelling and bearing them backward, they resolved, in accordance we believe with what had been previously arranged by the King, to perform a movement which ultimately was most successful.[7] Selecting among themselves the man or men deputed by Bruce to direct them, for an office of that kind regularly falls to the most skilful, they gathered together all the poles and straight young trees stript of branches they could procure, and fastening to the upper end of each either a sheet or a piece of coloured linen, such as could be supplied, for the spare clothing of the army was there, they formed themselves into ranks and columns, and, appearing in hostile array, came marching over the edge of the hill, sounding their horns in wild clamour, directly down to the battle-field.[8] Except for some natural trees or bushes, as there were scarcely any undulations of the ground, the whole course of their progress was observed by every opposing Englishman not engaged in actual conflict, and the sight apparently of a fresh and powerful army hastening to assist

---

[7] 'At a distance, in a valley, lay fifteen thousand followers of the army, whom the king dared not bring into the field, but whom he instructed to show themselves in the heat of the conflict as a new army hastening to the aid of their countrymen.'—*Lingard*, vol. iii. p. 21.

[8] 'Ane off thaim selwyn that war thar
    Capitane of thiam all thai maid.
And schetis, that war sumdele brad,
Thai festnyt in steid off baneris,
Apon lang treys and speris:
And said that thai wald se the fycht;
And help their lordis at thair mycht.'
                                         *Barbour*, p. 260.

the Scots, spread dismay and terror everywhere among them. On approaching the throng of battle, the gillies shouted to the full extent of their voices, 'Slay, slay! upon them hastily!' and the struggle became more and more deadly. By this time the English, who had fought face to face with the Scots from the commencement of the battle till now, were driven down towards the Bannock, yet they preserved their front manfully, dealing their blows, as if through despair, with tremendous effect, while behind, their fellow-countrymen were still so massed together that no space was left for retreat. On seeing the accession, however, of numbers to the Scottish ranks, astonishment and fear began to unnerve their resolution, while the gillies seized such weapons as were at hand, or could be caught from the dead and dying around them, and, uniting with the infantry, struck down whoever of their opponents they could reach.[9] The Scottish cavalry began now to perform a most important part, for whenever an opening occurred in the ranks of the English, these horsemen pressed forward among them, and made immense slaughter. About this

---

[9] 'And Inglis men, that ruschyt war
Throuch forss of fycht, as I said ar,
Quhen thai saw cummand, with sic a cry,
Towart thaim sic a cumpany,
That thaim thoucht wele als mony war,
As that wes fechtand with thaim thar;
And thai befor had nocht thaim sene;
Than, wit ye weill, with outyn wene,
Thai war abaysit sa gretumly,
That the best and the mast hardy,
That war in till thair ost that day,
Wald with thair mensk haf bene away.'
*Barbour*, p. 261.

time the Earl of Gloucester, in an attempt to turn the tide of battle, rode fiercely upon the advancing Scots, and, without being duly supported by his own followers, fell, pierced by the Scottish spears.[10] Bruce now perceiving how the ranks of the enemy were giving way, raised his war cry, and all those who were with him, animated by the prospect of victory, united with all their might in dealing destruction upon the reeling crowds before them.[11] During the whole period that the English were driven back, till the stream was reached, and even then, from the site of Park Mill to that of Chartershall, a series of desperate encounters would appear to have taken place. Barbour observes the Bannock was so bridged over with drowned horses and men that they who wished to cross it might

---

[10] *Tytler*, vol i. p 274.
[11] 'The king Robert, be thair relying,
Saw thai war ner at discomfiting,
And his ensenye gan hely cry.
Than, with thaim off his cumpany,
Hys fayis he pressyt sa fast that day,
[Thai] wer in till sa gret effray,
That thai left place ay mar and mar.
For all the Scottis men that thar war,
Quhen thai saw thaim eschew the fycht,
Dang on thaim with all thair mycht;
That thai scalyt thaim in troplys ser,
And till discomfitur war ner.
And sum off thaim fled all planly.
Bot thai, that wycht war and hardy,
That schame lettyt to ta the flycht,
At gret myscheiff mantemyt the fycht,
And stythly in the stour gan stand.'
*Barbour*, pp. 261-2

have done so dry-footed.[12]  At last, confounded, or overcome with alarm, terror, and amazement, whole squadrons of the English now betook themselves to flight. The battle was at length won, Scotland had conquered, and England was compelled to suffer an ignominious defeat.

---

[12] ' And Bannokburne, betuix the brays,
    Off men, off hors, swa stekyt wais,
    That, apon drownyt hors and men,
    Men mycht pass dry owt our it then.'
Barbour, p. 263.

We question the accuracy of this statement in one point only, for whether man or beast be drowned, they are generally found in deep water; hence, if the stream was so choked up, it must have been by men and horses who were killed and not drowned.

## CHAPTER XI.

### FLIGHT OF THE ENGLISH.

> Day glimmers on the dying and the dead,
> The cloven cuirass, and the helmless head,
> The war-horse masterless is on the earth
> And that last gasp hath burst his bloody girth;
> And near, yet quivering with what life remain'd,
> The heel that urg'd him and the hand that rein'd
> BYRON.

WE may readily conceive the astonishment and agonising feelings at this time of the English King. It is said that on the crisis of the fight, when the Scots were likely to win, he attempted to ride forward with or without his body guard, that he might dye his steel in the blood of the Scots;[1] but it is more likely he was held back by those

---

[1] Could we attach credit to the words of Patrick Gordon, King Edward rushed into the throng, and fought with the bravery which characterised his race, for he killed the Earl of Strathearn and his son, beside other knights whose names are not recorded.

> 'Their angry King
>     bravely from his Troops doth forth advance,
>         *       *       *       *
>   And there were killed by his princely Hand
>   Seven valiant Knights whose names hath Time forgot.
>         *       *       *       *
>   Strathern's old Earl there dy'd beneath his Brand
>   Whose Son with Sorrow prick'd, with Fury hot
>     Did fiercely him assail, but all in vain;
>     Death made him soon forget his Father's Pain'
> Gordon, p. 201

around him; and when at last De Valence, Earl of Pembroke, saw that the chance of victory was over and danger at hand, he seized the King's bridle and led him unwillingly away from the sickening scene.² Sir Giles de Argentine, true to his trust, whose lofty conception of knightly honour would not allow him to depart a fugitive from a stricken field, accompanied the monarch till he thought him safely away from danger, and then observing it was not his wont to fly from battle, wished him, 'God speed!' Turning his horse again to the field, he spurred forward, and shouting his war cry, 'An Argentine! An Argentine!' he encountered several horsemen and the infantry under Sir Edward Bruce, where he gallantly fell as became a brave and heroic knight. His loss was deplored by the Scots as well as the English, for he was accounted the third best knight in Christendom.³

---

² ' And ȝeyt haiff Ik hard som men say,
That of Walence Schir Aymer,
When he the feld saw wencusyt ner,
Be the reyngye led away the king,
Agayne his will, fra the fechting.'—*Barbour*, p. 262.

³ ' And quhen Schyr Gylis the Argenté
Saw the king thus, and his menye,
Schap thaim to fley sa spedyly,
He come rycht to the king in hy,
And said ; 'Schyr, sen it is sua
' That ye thusgat your gat will ga,
' Hawys gud day ! for agayne will I :
' Yeyt fled I neuir sekyrly.
' And I cheyss her to bid and dey,
' Than for to lyve schamly, and fley.'
Hys bridill, but mar abad,
He turnyt ; and agayne he rade,
And on Eduuard the Bruyss rout,

Panic-struck at the terrible calamity, and scarcely knowing what to do or where to go, the King of England, accompanied by his bishops, and having five hundred of his principal nobility around him,[4] rode at last direct to Stirling, by the nearest approach, and ascending to the castle, sought instant admittance.[5] Sir Philip Mowbray

---

> That wes sa sturdy, and sa stout,
> As drede off nakyn thing had he,
> He prikyt, cryand, 'The Argenté!'
> And thai with spuris swa him met,
> And swa fele speris on him set,
> That he and hors war chargyt swa,
> That bathe till the erd gan ga:
> And in that place thar slane wes he.
> Off hys deid wes rycht gret pité.
> He wes the thrid best knycht, perfay,
> That men wyst lywand in his day.
> He did mony a fayr journé.
> On Saryzynys thre derenyeys faucht he:
> And, in till ilk derenye off tha,
> He wencussyt Saryzynys twa.
> His gret worschip tuk thar ending'
> *Barbour*, pp. 262-3.

[4] Hugh de Lespencer, 'that cowardly bird of prey,' as Hailes calls him, quoting from Moore, was also of the number.

[5] 'And quhen the king of Ingland
> Saw his men fley, in syndry place,
> And saw his fayis rout, that was
> Worthyn sa wycht, and sa hardy,
> That all his folk war halyly
> Sa stonayit, that thai had na mycht
> To stynt thair fayis in the fycht;
> He was abaysyt sa gretumly,
> That he and his cumpany,
> Fyve hundre, armyt all at rycht,
> In till a frusch all tok the flycht,
> And to the castell held thair way.'—*Barbour*, p. 262

observed the fortress was at his monarch's will, but if he came within, he would undoubtedly be taken prisoner, for none in all England could either rescue him or render help. Whereupon he advised him to retain his knights by him, and wind round beneath the Park, so as to get away from the strife, in which case none would be able to do him injury. Hereupon he departed, taking his way beneath the castle, past the Round Table, and below the east side of the Park, on the direct road to Linlithgow, with the utmost speed.[6] Sir James Douglas, who perceived his flight, besought King Robert to allow him to give chase, which was granted, but as large numbers of the English were still near, no more than about sixty mounted horsemen could be spared for the pursuit.[7]

---

[6] ' Bot Philip the Mowbray said him till;
' The castell, Schyr, is at your will.
' Bot cum ye in it, ye sall se
' That ye sall sone assegyt be.
' And thar sall nane of Ingland
' To mak yow rescourss tak on hand.
' And, but rescours, may na castell
' Be haldyn lang, ye wete this wele.
' Tharfor comfort yow, and rely
' Your men about yow rycht starkly;
' And haldis about the Park your way,
' Rycht als sadly as ye may.
' For I trow that nane sall haff mycht,
' That chassys, with sa fele to fycht.'
And his consaill thai haff doyne.'—*Barbour*, p. 264.
See also Note 17, p. 31, *supra*.

[7] ' For Schyr James lord of Douglas
Come to the king, and askyt the chace;
And he gaff him it, but abaid.
Bot all to few of hors he haid:

When King Edward quitted the field, and the royal banner of England was borne away, any resistance on the side of her sons was hopeless, and, depressed by the awful calamity which was imminent, each man endeavoured to fly for safety, so that an incredible number were slain. Of those who remained longest on the field the slaughter was immense, for, being without the slightest means of resistance, they were stricken down and destroyed[8] on every side. But parties of the Scots intent on plunder, instead of chasing the enemy, preferred to gather spoil wherever it could be found, and they rifled the slain, besides collecting what booty they could acquire in the English camp, thereby allowing numbers to escape.[9] Many men of rank, as a means of safety, threw off their surcoats and armour, whereby their speed should be increased, and they would not attract attention, and fled half naked over the country in the direction of England. A large body of the fugitives,

---

He had nocht in hys rout sexty.
The quhethir he sped him hastely
The way eftyr the king to ta '—*Barbour*, p 265.

Lord Hailes agrees with Barbour as to the number of horsemen with which Douglas gave chase to the fugitives, though Buchanan and Hollinshed increase it to four hundred

[8] 'Ik hard neuir quhar, in na contré
Folk at sua gret myscheiff war stad.
On ane sid thai thair fayis had,
That slew thaim doun for owten mercy.'
*Barbour*, pp 263-4.

[9] 'Very few of the flying army would have escaped with life and liberty if many of the Scotch soldiers had not preferred the plunder of the English camp (where they found an immense booty) to the pursuit of their enemies.'—*Mon Malms.* p. 152, quoted by *Henry*, vol. vii p 143.

who had kept together, after they passed the spot where Bannockburn House now stands, made an attempt to check the pursuers, but without avail, and the place where it is said they all fell is still known in the locality by the name of the 'Bloody Faulds.' Other companies, diverging from the line wherein the pursuit was chiefly made, and, hastening down to the carse, endeavoured to cross the Forth, in which many of them were drowned.[10] It has been already stated that Bannockburn at that time, below Chartershall, ran deeply amid slake and earth, so that many who lingered on the field, and had escaped slaughter by the lower orders of the Scots, were also overwhelmed in the sluggish stream.[11]

Among the English nobility who fled and were not of the number who accompanied the King, was the Earl of Hereford, who took a southern direction, with many of his

---

[10] 'And fra Schyr Aymer with the king
Was fled, wes nane that durst abid;
Bot fled, scalyt on ilka sid.
And thair fayis thaim pressyt fast.
Thai war, to say suth, swa agast,
And fled sa fast, rycht effrayitly,
That off thaim a full gret party
Fled to the watre of Forth; and thar
The mast part off thaim drownyt war.'
*Barbour*, p. 263.

[11] 'Sua that sum slayne, sum drownyt war:
Mycht nane eschap that cuir come thar.'
*Barbour*, p. 264.

The channel of the Bannock, ere it enters the valley below Milton, has been deepened considerably since the time of the battle. There is now, and has been for a lengthened period, a gradual descent in its course, for the bridge which spans the stream, near the above village, has been widened on two several occasions.

I

followers, and knowing the country, went direct to the castle of Bothwell, which was held by his own countryman, Sir Walter Gilbertson, who took him in over the walls, with fifty of his dependants.[12] The remainder of the fugitives escaped towards England, but only about a fourth of the number reached the Border land in safety, the others being either killed or made prisoners.[13] Another large company who attempted to escape by flight were Welchmen who had accompanied Maurice de Berkeley, but being almost naked, for they wore light linen covering only, many were captured, and still more slain.[14] Of those who were

---

[12] 'The erle of Herfurd fra the mellé
Departyt, with a gret mengné :
And straucht to Bothwell tok the vai,
That than in the Ingliss mennys fay
Was, and haldyn as [a] place of wer.
Schyr Waltre Gilbertson wes ther
Capitane, and it had in ward.
The erle of Herfurd thiddyrward
Held, and wes tane in our the wall,
And fyfty of his men with all,
And set in howssis sindryly ;'—*Barbour*, p 265.

[13] 'The lave went towart Ingland.
Bot off that rout, I tak on hand,
The thre partis war slane or tane.
The lave with gret payn hame are gane'
*Barbour*, pp 265-6

[14] 'Schyr Mawrice, alsua, the Berclay,
Fra the gret bataill held hys way,
With a gret rout off Walis men.
Quhar euir thai yeid men mycht thaim ken,
For thai wele ner all nakyt war,
Or lynnyn clathys had but mar.
Thai held thair way in full gret hy.
Bot mony off thair cumpany,

## FLIGHT OF THE ENGLISH. 115

left with life, and knowing that no mercy would be shown them in flying towards Falkirk, the chief portion—and a large number they were—sought their way northward, and took refuge on and around the crags to the west and north of Stirling Castle, and almost covered these rocky precipices.[15] Indeed, with other fugitives, they were so numerous that King Robert entertained some doubt they might rally again, wherefore he kept his good men near him to repress any assault, for which cause he could not afford Douglas a sufficient number of horse to pursue King Edward, and accordingly the latter got safely away.[16]

One may conceive the consternation of those men, women, and youths, who were left with the provision-waggons, etc., when they beheld their monarch with his nobles flying past them on horseback at full speed for life. Mile after mile this must have been the case, and the

---

      Or thai till Ingland come, war tane ;
      And mony als off thaim war slayne.'—*Barbour*, p. 266.

[15] ' Bot to the castell, that wes ner,
      Off Strewilline fled sic a mengye,
      That it war wondre for to se.
      For the craggis all helyt war
      About the castell, her and thar,
      Off thaim, that for strenth of that sted,
      Thiddyrwart to warand fled.'—*Barbour*, p. 266.

[16] ' And for thai war sa fele, that thar
      Fled wndre the castell war,
      The king Robert, that wes wytty,
      Held in his gud men ner him by,
      For drede that riss agayne suld thai.
      This wass the causs, forsuth to say,
      Quhar throuch the King of Ingland
      Eschapyt hame in till his land.'—*Barbour*, p. 266.

sight would indicate to them the hard fate they would probably have to undergo ere they could hope to set foot upon their own land. It was a most exciting chase. While Sir James Douglas was pursuing King Edward past the Torwood he met Sir Lawrence Abernethy with twenty horsemen, who had come with the intention of assisting the English, but on observing the result of the battle he swore to be leal and true to Bruce, and joined Douglas in the pursuit.[17] On passing Linlithgow the Scottish horse approached the fugitives so near that they might almost have come into conflict, but the latter were so numerous that the pursuers deemed it imprudent to stay them in their flight. Keeping, however, close upon them, they watched their chance; and when any one of the English lingered or was left behind, even a short way, he was certain to be either killed or made prisoner. King Edward, aware of his danger, vowed to God or the Virgin that if he might escape with life he would build a house to the Carmelite or White Friars, in which he would place

---

[17] 'Now will we of the Lord of Douglas
Tell, how that he folowit the chas.
He had to quhone in his cumpany;
Bot he sped him in full gret hy.
And as he throuch the Torwod fur,
Sa met he ridand on the mur
Schyr Laurence off Abyrnethy,
That, with twenty-four in cumpany,
Come for till help the Englismen ;
For he was Ingliss man yet then.
But quhen he hard how that it wes,
He left the Inglis mennys pess ;
And to the lord Dowglas rycht thar
For to be lele and trew he swar.'—*Barbour*, p. 270.

twenty-four brethren; and, in fulfilment of this promise, though in opposition to the advice of one of his parasites, the younger Spencer, Oriel College in Oxford, was erected.[18]

At Winchburgh, a small village eleven miles west of Edinburgh, the English halted to feed their horses, and the pursuers did the same, but, speedily mounting, the former pursued their way direct to the castle of Dunbar, where King Edward and fifteen Earls in his company[19] were received by Patrick Dunbar, Earl of March, leaving their horses behind them, which were immediately seized by the Scots. The remainder of the English held onward towards Berwick, but as they were numerous, preserving their array and threatening defiance in case of interruption, Douglas found it necessary to allow them to depart.[20] It is said he left a party of horsemen to capture the King in case he should venture by land to his own kingdom. But when King Edward recovered from his bodily fatigue, his friend and host, the Earl of March,[21] taking from him a

---

[18] *Stow*, p. 217.      [19] *Hollinshed*, p. 219.

[20] 'The lave, that lewyt thar without,
Adressyt thaim in till a rout,
And till Berwik held straucht thair way
In route.'—*Barbour*, p. 272.

[21] 'Patrike Dūbarre, erle of Marche, that daye
To Kyng Edward was leege mā lōg afore
To his father, and trewe had been alwaye,
Sent Kyng Edward to Barwik; but, therefore,
He toke of hym a relesse for euermore
Of his seruice that due was to the [his] croune,
Anentes Kyng Bruys to execute [excuse] his treason.'
                           *Hardyng*, p. 306.

This release, with other documents of Scottish History, Har-

release of his service, got him conveyed in a boat, with a few of his chief men, by sea from Dunbar, either to Berwick or Bambrough, which he reached in safety.[22]

---

dyng says, he afterwards delivered into the treasury of King Henry the Fifth, at Boys Vincent, in France, for which he received the manor or villa of Godyngton in Oxfordshire, and which subsequently came into possession of the Queen.

[22] Barbour says he went in 'a bate be se to Bawmburgh,' while Turner observes that, 'getting into a ship, he sailed precipitately to Berwick.'

## CHAPTER XII.

#### LIBERAL TREATMENT OF PRISONERS.

> When, without stratagem,
> But in plain shock, and even play of battle,
> Was ever known so great and little loss,
> On one part and on th' other?—SHAKESPEARE.

In relating the above incidents subsequent to the battle, we are impressed with the apparent lack of precaution on the part of King Edward, his advisers, and the English nobility, to whose charge the expedition to Scotland was entrusted. Blindly confiding in their own strength, and deeming that every obstacle would give way before them, no arrangement whatever seems to have been made either to ward off danger or provide for safety in the event of defeat. When the Scots gained the battle, had the English, who were under arms, withdrawn from the field, and kept together in regular order, presenting a barrier of defence, and retreating as well as they could in front of their pursuers, conveying the most valuable portion of their provision and baggage with them, how different had the result been, as to the loss of both life and property. Whenever King Edward quitted the field, the whole remaining divisions of the army who fought for him, being altogether undefended, fled, and were captured, or cut down without mercy, whereas large numbers, under more prudent guidance, might, unscathed, have reached England, and lived to a good old age.

When the battle was decided, and the English who were unwounded and at liberty had left the field, the Scots forthwith commenced to seize upon such spoil as they could secure. Many, indeed, who had previously endured much privation, acquired vast wealth, which enabled them to assume a high station during the remainder of their lives.[1] The King, in the meantime, having sent a goodly battalion of armed men to secure the large number of English who had fled to the crags at Stirling Castle, they speedily accomplished the object of their mission, and made them prisoners.[2] On returning they were also allowed to join the others in plundering the slain, which they did, stripping the bodies, and many secured much spoil. It was a marvellous sight to behold the vast multitude of those who had fallen, for, of our ancient English families, it is presumed that scarcely one could be named who had not an ancestor either killed or made prisoner in the battle, or in the flight from that fatal field.[3]

---

[1] 'Quhen that the feld sa clene was maid
Off Inglis men, that nane abaid,
The Scottis men sone tuk in hand
Off tharis all that euir thai fand;
That mony men mychty wes maid
Off the riches that thai thar haid.'
*Barbour*, pp. 266-7.

[2] 'The king send a gret cumpany
Wp to the crag, thaim till assaile
That war fled fra the gret battaill:
And thai thaim yauld for owtyn debate,
And in hand has tane thaim fute hate'
*Barbour*, p 267.

[3] 'If the list (of the slain and those made prisoners, as supplied by the continuator of Trivet's *Annals*) were complete, most of

## TREATMENT OF PRISONERS.

We believe the exact number of the English who were slain on the field and in flight, and those who were taken prisoners, cannot possibly be ascertained. Following our best authorities, we would say that about thirty thousand were slain in battle, and fell as fugitives on the way to their own country. Nearly five hundred of the chief men accompanied the King and escaped, but about two hundred knights were killed on the field[4] and seven hundred esquires. Taking the above statement as approximating to the truth, while King Edward brought one hundred thousand men to the field, allowing for a few thousands of prisoners, something less than sixty-five thousand would get away with life, and this may be near an average of what has occurred, with regard to numbers only, in very many battles from the earliest date to the present time. The servants and camp-followers are not comprised in this statement. Many of these undoubtedly would be killed, while others would be fortunate enough to escape.

Among the nobles who were killed, the most illustrious was Gilbert de Clare, Earl of Gloucester. He was nephew to the King, his mother being Joan of Acre, daughter to Edward the First.[5] When the ranks of the English gave way towards the close of the battle, Gloucester as has been said, spurred forward against the Scots, and not being duly supported by his train of five hundred men-at-arms, a

---

the English families would find the names of their predecessors among the slain, or among the prisoners at Bannockburn.'—*Hailes*, Note, vol. ii. p. 51.

[4] ' Twa hundre payr off spuris reid
War tane of knychtis that war deid.'
*Barbour*, p. 267.

[5] *Dugdale*, vol. i. p. 216.

few of whom might have rescued him, he was instantly dismounted and slain. King Robert Bruce being related to the Earl,[6] mourned in secret for his death, and causing his body to be conveyed to a neighbouring church, it was waked there all the night. Sir Robert Clifford, another gallant warrior, who encountered Randolph previous to the battle, but without success, was also found among the slain. The same honour was bestowed on his remains that was awarded to the Earl of Gloucester, and both bodies, free of any ransom, were sent to King Edward at Berwick, to be interred in England with the honours due to their birth and valour.[7] Among others, Lord William le Mareshall had also fallen, and Sir Edmund de Mauley, High Steward of England, was discovered drowned in Bannockburn.[8] Of the other men of rank who fell, the attentive reader is referred to the appendix, where a number of names are recorded.[9]

On the side of Scotland the loss of men must also have been considerable, for it is probable the Scottish chroniclers, who state the number to be about four thousand, intentionally kept the figure low.[10] Of the chief men, only two were killed, Sir William Vipont and Sir Walter Ross. The latter seems to have been an especial favourite with Sir Edward Bruce, who made much lamentation when he

---

[6] His grandfather, Robert, the competitor for the crown, married Isabel, daughter of Gilbert de Clare, seventh Earl of Gloucester, consequently she was his grandmother —*Banks*, vol. i. p. 138.

[7] *Walsingham*, vol. i. p. 142. *Tyrrell*, vol. iii. p. 261. *Hailes*, vol. ii. p 52

[8] *Stow*, p. 216.     [9] See Note C.

[10] *Hollinshed*, at p. 219, mentions that about four thousand fell.

heard of his death.[11] When, however, the battle was honourably won, King Robert and his company were most joyful on the occasion, being highly delighted at their good fortune. They thanked God that of his grace He had enabled them to preserve in their own land all they held hallowed and dear, and, as they required rest, after every arrangement for safety had been completed, they accordingly withdrew, each to the place where he might enjoy repose.

Next morning early, as King Robert went forth to survey the battle-field, an English knight, Sir Marmaduke Twenge,[12] who, at the close of the conflict seeing no chance of escape, had hid himself amid some bushes, came forward, and bending on his knee, presented himself before Bruce. The King knew him at once, and giving him welcome, asked to whom he was prisoner. 'To none, save to your Majesty,' said the knight. 'Then I receive you,' observed Bruce, and forthwith treated him with much courtesy. He dwelt with the King for a time, and the latter not only sent him to England free of ransom but bestowed upon

---

[11] Some improper intimacy would appear to have existed between Sir Edward Bruce and Isabella, sister of Ross, but the story is not clearly authenticated. Sir Edward married the sister of David de Strathbogie, Earl of Athole, whom, it is said, he slighted; and her brother, in revenge for the deed, assaulted the King's head-quarters at Cambuskenneth, when the two armies were about to engage, and slew the guard with the commander Sir William Keith. In 1317 Athole went over to the service of England, and in 1323 a sentence of forfeiture was issued against him.—*Kerr*, vol. i. pp. 490-1.

[12] He was a noted warrior, having conducted himself most gallantly against Wallace in the battle of Stirling.

him handsome gifts.[13] Moreover, Sir Philip Mowbray also sought the King, and yielding to him the castle of Stirling, entered into an agreement to serve him in the capacity of a true subject, which he performed faithfully to the end of his life.[14] It also occurred that Ralph de Monthermer, who had married Joan of Acre, mother to the Earl of Gloucester, fled along with the King on his way to Dunbar, but, falling behind, was taken prisoner. He bore the target, or, as Stow calls it, the ' the shield or seale,' belonging to King Edward, but when he was brought before Bruce, from the accidental familiarity which once existed between them at the court of England, he, according to Dugdale, ' was pardoned his fine for redemption,[15] who thereupon returned into England, and brought the King's target which had been taken in that fight, but prohibited the use thereof.'[16] Roger de Northburge, keeper of the King's signet, and his two clerks, Roger de Wikenfelde and Thomas de Switon, were captured, together with the

---

[13] ' Schyr Marmeduk the Twenge he hycht.
He raykyt till the king all rycht,
And halyst him apon his kne.
' Welcum, Schyr Marmeduk,' said he ;
' To quhat man art thow presoner ?'—
' To nane,' he said, ' bot to yow her.
' I yeld me at your will to be '—
' And I ressave the, Schyr,' said he.
Than gert he tict him curtasly.
He duelt lang in his company :
And syne till Ingland him send he,
Arayit weile, but ransoun fre ,
And geff him gret gyftis tharto.'—*Barbour*, p. 269.
[14] *Barbour*, p 313   [15] *i.e.* Was set at liberty free of ransom
[16] *Dugdale*, vol. i. p. 217.

said seal, which was delivered to Bruce, but he restored the signet to Edward on condition it should not again be used. The King of England thereby caused a new one to be made, and, to distinguish it from the other, entitled it his privy seal.[17]

It has been stated that Sir John Menteith, who betrayed Wallace, was liberated from prison on condition, his sons-in-law, influential men, being surety, that in the event of a battle he should fight in the front ranks of the Scottish King. This duty Menteith performed at Bannockburn so well and so bravely, that by his prowess, he not only procured pardon for his previous base behaviour, but received from Bruce a bountiful reward for his service, and continued a faithful subject to the end of his life.[18]

King Robert, when a reasonable time had elapsed, gave orders that the bodies of the lords and nobility of England who were slain, so far as they could be recognised, should be honourably consigned to holy ground. This might be difficult, as both rich and poor, the former especially so, would be stripped and left almost naked on the field. Besides, the alteration of the features by violent death, might render it almost impossible to ascertain several of the men of note who had fallen. The King also commanded that large pits should be dug on the field, wherein the scattered heaps of common people who had fallen might be decently interred.[19]

---

[17] *Trivet*, p. 15. 'Bruce was more generous than Edward I., who placed the fragments of the great seal of Scotland in the Treasury of England.'—*Kerr*, vol. i. p. 493.

[18] *Buchanan*, vol. i. p. 428; *Hollinshed*, pp. 220-1.

[19] 'And the gret lordis, that he fand
  Dede in the feld, he gert bery

The King made the towers of Stirling Castle his place of residence for a time, and, having learned that the Earl of Hereford with his chief followers had taken refuge in Bothwell Castle, he dispatched his brother Edward with a sufficient force to that fortress, and after a short siege, the captain, Sir Walter Gilbertson, capitulated, agreeing to surrender Hereford with the other warriors into the hands of the King.[20] The Earl was accordingly sent to Bruce, who received him with respect and courtesy. By arrangement he was permitted to go to England without ransom, but in exchange for him, Elizabeth, the Queen of Bruce, daughter to the Earl of Ulster, Christian, the sister of Bruce, and Marjory the King's daughter,[21] Robert Wisheart,

---

   In haly place honorabilly ;
   And the lave syne, that dede war thar,
   Into gret pyttis erdyt war.'—*Barbour*, p. 273.

None of these pits have yet been discovered. There are clumps of trees growing in lowish moist places over the field where it is supposed cottages once stood, and these appeared to the author as likely spots of sepulture. Still one or more of these depositories of mortality may yet be found. The skeleton of Robert Bruce in the church of Dunfermline was almost entire, when discovered in 1818; and south-west of Brankston, Andrew Rankin of that village, about 1820, cut a drain three and a half feet deep over a large pit of the bones of many of the heroes who fell at Flodden.

See the author's account of the battle of Flodden in *Archæologia Æliana*, New Series, vol. iii. p. 197.

[20] By the industry of Joseph Stevenson, Esq., of the Rolls Office, a list of those who were taken will be found by the curious reader in the Appendix to that gentleman's edition of *Chronicon de Lanercost*, printed for the Bannatyne Club in 1839, pp. 417-8.

[21] Marjory had been given in charge to Henry Percy, and she and Walter de Morrene were kept in the castle of Newcastle-upon-Tyne.—*Chron. de Lan.*, Note, p. 418; *Fœdera*, vol. ii. p. 1014.

Bishop of Glasgow, who was blind,[22] and the youthful Earl of Mar, nephew to the King, were set free,[23] and returned to their own country.[24] The English, it would appear, had slight value by way of barter, for about the 20th November following, John de Segrave, an English baron who had been captured, was exchanged for five Scottish prisoners, David de Lindesay, Andrew Moray, Thomas de Morrain, Reginald de Lindesay, and Alexander, his brother.[25]

---

[22] 'Robert Wisheart, Bishop of Glasgow in 1306, held the castle of Coupar in Fife against the English. He was made prisoner there, arrayed in armour, and in that uncanonical garb was conducted to the castle of Nottingham.'—*Hailes*, vol. ii. p. 13.

[23] 'The young Earl of Mar, nephew to the first wife of Robert Bruce, was imprisoned in 1306, but not chained on account of his tender years.'—*Fœdera*, vol. ii. p. 1013; *Hailes*, vol. ii. p. 17.

[24] 'And syne to Bothwell send he
Schyr Eduuard with a gret menye;
For thar wes than send him word
That the rich erle off Herford,
And othyr mychty als, wer ther.
Swa tretyt he with Schyr Walter,
That erle, and castell, and the lave,
In Schyr Eduuardis hand he gave.
And till the king the erle send he,
That gert him rycht weill yemyt be:
Quhill at the last thai tretyt sua
That he till Ingland hame suld ga,
For owtyn paying of ransoune, fre;
And that for him suld changyt be
Byschap Robert that blynd was mad;
And the queyne, that thai takyn had
In presoune, as befor said I;
And hyr douchtre dame Maiory.'
*Barbour*, pp. 273-4.

[25] *Fœdera*, vol. iii. p. 502; *Taylor*, vol. i. p. 139.

## CHAPTER XIII.

#### BENEFICIAL RESULTS OF THE BATTLE.

We cannot over-estimate the value of Bannockburn to us a people. Had we been subdued never would we have mixed kindly in union with England. We should have been like Ireland, full of heart-burnings, jealousies, reluctance, hatred, strife, misery. Bannockburn stamped and sealed us as a people with a national history. After that we could well afford to be magnanimous, generous, and friendly in every arrangement with the great sister nation whom we had so triumphantly repelled. A broad calm of conscious dignity, a liberal national atmosphere, thus settled for ever around the glad head of Scotland.—THOMAS AIRD.

AMONG the lower ranks of the English who were unable to escape was Robert Baston, the Carmelite friar,[1] already mentioned. On being taken, and the aim of his mission told to King Robert Bruce, the churchman was desired to sing to another tune, with which he complied; and the result of his poetic ability is a Latin composition on the battle, consisting chiefly of rhyming hexameters. The piece is preserved by Bower in his continuation of Fordun's *Scotichronicon*.[2]

All that the King and the English host had brought with them—beautiful horses, flocks of cattle, provisions of

---

[1] From the vow made by King Edward during his flight to build a house for the White friars, he seems to have been very partial to that fraternity.

[2] Vol. ii. pp. 251-5.

## RESULTS OF THE BATTLE. 129

corn and wine in abundance, sumptuous clothing from the royal wardrobe and other sources, gay pavilions, splendid armour for the nobles and knights, vessels and utensils of silver and gold of vast value and exquisite workmanship, with the money chests and coin for the payment of the army, all fell into the hands of the Scots.[3] Cows, pigs, and poultry, with waggons, horses, and baggage of every description, must have extended almost from Foot o' Green on towards Falkirk. The loss to England amounted, we are told, to two hundred thousand pounds, the value of which, according to Tytler,[4] may be estimated at about three millions of our present money.[5] Besides this, the ransoms paid by prisoners for their freedom would realise a very large sum, which is computed almost to equal the value of the plunder secured on the battle-field and in the

---

[3] 'O day of vengeance and of misfortune! day of disgrace and perdition! unworthy to be included in the circle of the year, which tarnished the fame of England, and enriched the Scots with the plunder of the precious stuffs of our nation to the extent of two hundred thousand pounds! Alas! of how many noble barons, and accomplished knights, and high-spirited young soldiers—of what a store of excellent arms, and golden vessels and costly vestments, did one short and miserable day deprive us?'—*Mon. Malms.*, p. 152. *Tytler's* Trans., vol. i. pp. 278-9.

[4] Vol. i. p. 279.

[5] The inquisitive reader may test the accuracy of this statement by the following extract:—' In the viii yere of the Kyng (1314) was a Parlement at London, where was a gret ordinauns to chepe vitaile, and it avayled not. It was ordeyned that a oxe fed with gresse schuld be seld for xviš.; a fatte oxe for xxiiiiš.; a fatte cow for xiiš.; a good swyn, to yere old, for xld.; a shep withouten wolle, for xiiiid; a fatte schep with wolle, xxd. * * a capon, iid.; a henne, id.; iiii dowes, id., and if ony man seld ony othir pris, the vitail be forfete to the Kyng.'—*Capgrave*, pp. 180-1.

K

English camp.⁶ Bruce dealt out the spoil most liberally to his faithful subjects, and so very equitably, that all expressed themselves satisfied; indeed the whole Scottish army was enriched by the victory.⁷ He also rewarded many of the nobles, who had done him good service, with possessions of a more permanent nature than money, and among the number Robert Fleming got the lands of Cumbernauld.⁸

Mention has been made of the two knights of Brabant, who were expelled from the English army on the night before the battle, and a reward set upon their heads by the King of England. They had been received by Bruce, and when he had leisure he bestowed on these men riches from the spoil gathered on the field, with which, on returning to their own land, they built a goodly house at Antwerp, calling it 'Scotland,' and causing a picture of Bruce, with the Scottish arms, to be set up thereon. The house afforded accommodation to Scotsmen from that time down, towards the close of the sixteenth century.⁹

The articles used in besieging towns and demolishing castles, which the English had also brought with them, were carefully preserved by the King, that they might be employed either against their former possessors, or other

---

⁶ 'They got little lesse monie and riches by ransoming of prisoners taken at this battell, than of spoile gotten in the fight, campe, and field.'—*Hollinshed*, p. 219.

⁷ 'The spoile was so great of gold, silver, and other jewels gotten in the field, that the whole number of the Scotish armie was made rich thereby.'—*Hollinshed*, p. 219.

⁸ Robert Fleming, for his faithful service, gat the landis of Cummernald.'—*Bellenden*, vol. ii. p 394.

⁹ *Bellenden*, vol ii pp. 394-5. *Hollinshed*, p. 220

enemies of Scotland.[10] Probably they were used shortly afterwards in throwing down the fortifications of Stirling Castle, for when the King had arranged all matters relating to the overthrow of the English, he caused the walls and towers of that stronghold to be levelled with the ground.[11] But out of all the property which the English left behind them, the rich stuffs and clothing were destined to be preserved for the greatest number of years. They were bestowed with other spoil to the cathedrals, the abbeys, and monasteries throughout the kingdom, as a thank-offering to God for the complete success with which the efforts of Bruce and his patriots had been crowned, in the deliverance from thraldom of their native land. Fashioned into altar-cloths, copes, and other sacred vestments, they would be regarded for several generations as relics of the memorable day on which Scotland achieved her freedom at Bannockburn.[12]

Allusion has been made to the servants of the English and the camp followers. We may suppose that these and the numbers who intended to reside in Scotland, expecting

---

[10] Bower, in his continuation of *Scotichronicon*, describing the result of the battle of Bannockburn, says 'all the English provisions fell into the hands of the Scots, with their petraries and shovels, rafters and mangonels, ladders and engines, pavilions and bell-tents, slings and bombards, and other machines of war.'— *Meyrick*, vol. i. p. 204.

[11] 'The castell, and the towris, syne
Rycht till the ground doune gert he myn.'
*Barbour*, p 273.

[12] 'The goldin and silkin claithis, of quhilkis King Edwardis palyonis war maid, war distribut amang the abbays of Scotland, to be vestamentis and frontallis to thair altaris; of quhilkis mony yit remanis to our days.'—*Bellenden*, vol. ii. pp. 393-4.

it to be conquered, would be subject to great suffering, for they were left in the midst of enemies who were stirred up to revenge by the wrongs they had endured from England, and were perhaps too ready, when the day of retribution came, to inflict punishment upon the innocent for the actions of the guilty. Some, probably, were wantonly butchered, others might suffer death in various ways, while many would find their position hard enough to undergo. Numbers might get away, for, if their clothing was scanty, and they had health, the season was favourable for escape. Even of those who endured much, compassion in calmer hours might follow, and it may be presumed that many a homely Scottish matron, touched with the wretchedness of the poor outcasts, afforded them relief in their wanderings, gave them food to eat, and administered to their wants, in the faith that they were acting up to the better and nobler impulses of our nature, and accordingly would not be without reward.

The result of the battle being remarkable considering the disparity of numbers on each side, the Church was not slow in imputing the good fortune of Scotland to the immediate interposition of heaven. On the evening before the battle, says the Canon of Aberdeen,[13] there came to the Abbey of Glastonbury, which at that time, like other religious houses, was open to receive strangers, two men in singular clothing, who asked to be accommodated for the night. The Abbot received them kindly, gave them good cheer, and, in the course of conversation, made inquiry who they were, and towards what quarter they were bound.

---

[13] *Hector Boece* per *Bellenden*, vol. ii. p. 394, and *Hollinshed*, p. 220.

They observed that, being servants of God, they were on the way to assist the Scots at Bannockburn. Next morning the chamberlain found they were gone before the gates were open, and the beds appointed for them were in the same condition as they had been left on the evening before. It was thereby believed these had been spiritual messengers sent from on high to succour the Scots in their righteous efforts against the unjust tyranny of England.

Likewise, from the same authority, we learn that on the same day the battle was fought, a knight, in bright shining armour, intimated to the inhabitants of Aberdeen how the Scottish army had gained a glorious victory over their enemies of England. Soon afterwards this warrior, mounted on horseback, was seen to pass over Pentland Firth. He was believed by the people to be Saint Magnus, Prince of Orkney, and thereby King Robert endowed the church of Orkney with five pounds annually, out of the customs of Aberdeen to purchase bread, wine, and wax for the use of the Abbey.

We are unable, even at this late period, to calculate the benefit which flowed to Scotland by the brave men, the most able and powerful of her whole people, who, under the direction of the greatest of her kings, fought and nobly accomplished the consummation of her liberties on this battle-field. Like the Greeks, fully aware of right and wrong, and aroused by their own heroic valour, these sons of freedom conquered here, and, though centuries since have come and gone, the event forms a sure step in the progress of civilisation, indicating that despotism must be subdued, and universal brotherhood be ultimately established over the whole globe. It follows that great men who have conferred renown on a country by which the people therein are elevated in the scale of humanity, have a memory green and flourishing, which survives age after age, as if they were still near, and had been known to us as intimate friends. Wallace and Bruce, Randolph and Douglas, cannot die, for we remain their debtors, and, by venerating their names, we ever hold them in grateful remembrance. To us, accordingly, it is a gratification highly intellectual to visit and walk over land once trode by heroes; and when we stand on the very spot whereon they performed the principal triumph of their lives, we feel it is man alone that can invest a place with glory, and consecrate it by his noble actions, so that all must regard it as hallowed ground. The soil, therefore, of that battle-field, though cultivated and divided into sections by walls or hedgerows, is sacred, and must ever remain so to the latest period of time. Thus, to every Scotsman who feels proud of his country, no locality in Europe can possibly have the power to operate more suggestively on his thoughts, or inspire him with more grateful adoration to the GREAT BEING who orders all things for good, than the solitary field of Bannockburn.

# ADDENDA.

### CONCLUDING REMARKS.

> Bannockburn was the best summer days' darg Scotland ever did. She put in the sickle and reaped a great harvest, which has filled her barns and fed her children with the food of freedom and stout-hearted exultation.—JOHN HILSON.

WE have not only heard it said, but a minor historian[1] has asked, 'what was the real gain to Scotland from Bannockburn, and would it not have been as well, since the whole island was to be ruled by one sceptre, if the union had taken place then as three centuries later?' We know the laws of the Plantagenets were equitable and beneficial, but had the arms of England gained the ascendancy at Bannockburn, the Scots under the one sceptre must have been considered and dealt with as a conquered people. Instead of this, when James the First came to occupy the English throne, the equality of both kingdoms had for many generations been established; and though Scotland was not so wealthy as the sister land, her sons were not behind their southern neighbours in arts, arms, and the other ennobling qualities which reflect honour on any country. Hence, when Scotland was united to England, the Scots, to their honour be it recorded, experienced neither abasement nor elevation by the change, whereas, had they in

---

[1] Thomas Keightley.

1314 been subdued, their position from that date had been of the most abject description.

All ancient records, including portions of the Historical Books of the Old Testament, the works of Herodotus, Thucydides, the accounts of the Roman Empire, and that of England even down to the Middle Ages, show that the shedding of human blood by the baser passions of man, by warfare and other unhallowed designs throughout the world, made it resemble a den of wild beasts. Some cessation might occasionally be made in wholesale slaughter, yet it must be admitted that the weaker and undefended portions of humanity, including both sexes, were, from the upper ranks, subject at all times to oppression, privation, and death. A gleam of improvement was thrown over this sombre prospect by the institution of chivalry and its ameliorating influences, still it only resembled the sunshine of a wintry day flickering on the surface of frost and snow. Safety from outward assault there was none, unless it were possible that a person of undoubted prowess could remain isolated from society, and by means of rock, wall, and his own weapons and skill, defend himself against all aggression.

If, therefore, we keep in view the increasing power of England subsequent to 1314, and the probable inability of Scotland ever again to take the field with any chance of success in recovering her independence, no worse evil could have befallen the latter country than to be vanquished at Bannockburn. England proved by her hostility against the Scots at the time what treatment they might expect from their lordly conquerors. It is not the province of the historian to conceive, Dante-like, the perilous condition of the people of the northern land thus deprived of their

## CONCLUDING REMARKS.

honour, yet we may affirm it would be one of great severity. Deprived of all that sweetens existence, humiliated, broken in heart and spirit, without hope of relief, and considering what they had to endure, death to the sufferers had often been welcome. Any Scotsman, under these circumstances, meeting with an Englishman, had been impressed with a sense of inferiority, and though indeed superior in some honourable qualities to the other, he and his descendants could only mourn over their state of degradation. Groanings, mutterings, and curses, would have arisen from every corner of Scotland; while the energy, the noble manliness, the strong desire for liberty, among her sons had been suppressed, and if possible stamped out by the domination of England. The hateful 24th of June, when it came annually round, had been to the Scots a day of wailing, sorrow, and despair, since it placed them in a condition of bondage, whence for ages they were unable to extricate themselves.

Thanks, however, be to Providence, Scotland maintained with the utmost fortitude her position against the foe, and nobly won the palm of victory. Nor did the sound of her exultation die away on the battle-field, or during the year of her fortunate struggle, but it was re-echoed for centuries, and will continue to be so over the length and breadth of her soil, telling her people to take heart and overcome all trial, for, like Paul, when confronted with the chief captain at Jerusalem, they can proudly say they were FREE-BORN. Remembering this, with resolute and undaunted courage to maintain what is right and reject what is wrong, we trust that should peril ensue, like their invincible ancestors they will withstand to the death any attempt to impose on their liberty.

Greece fought for this boon and conquered, but in a few generations her hard-won wreath of honour withered away. Scotland still preserves the priceless pearl in her diadem, and, though only a small province compared with the nations of the earth who are without that blessing, she exhibits a glorious lesson to the world that—

'Who would be free themselves must strike the blow.'

Defensive war only is reconcilable with justice, and when the rights of a community are threatened either by a tyrant or a foreign foe, it then becomes a sacred duty that they arm themselves and defy to the uttermost the insolent oppressor. Recent events prove it were well for all, if every despot was either destroyed like a wild beast, or immured in a cell and cut off from all connection with his fellow-men. It is on them he means to prey, their blood is to be shed, and their means wasted without hope of return on his account, while his aim is to hold them in bondage, and use them so that others also may be brought under his detestable sway. The peace of the world is evidently endangered when the sole command of any kingdom is vested in the power of a single individual such as King or Emperor, though surrounded by counsellors; so that, for absolute security, a representative system of authority, founded on the widest possible basis, is preferable, whereby the will of the people, paramount at all times, can be brought to bear freely on every essential part of executive administration. Accordingly, we believe that in each enlightened community there is a tendency towards this form of Government, and it seems to realise the truth of the poet's lines that the time will come

'When man to man the warld o'er
Shall brothers be for a' that.'

We do therefore trust that better times will dawn on the world. Education, pursued till its fruit tell upon the multitude, will do much to open up a brighter prospect, for we have faith to believe that, by its influence, the prevalence of sober judgment, and consequent readiness to adjust human wrong, will cause devastating wars ultimately to cease. The inhabitants, however, of any land who aspire to be free must know how to estimate their own weight and power, must be able judiciously to regulate themselves, and, moreover, must be true and just men, otherwise liberty would be license to evil, and they would abuse the high privileges they seek to obtain. It is only by the regular exercise of self-control, and practice of the Christian virtues, whereby ' on earth peace, goodwill toward men' are secured, that the people of any country can rise to greatness, or share to the full in the blessings that are enjoyed in a free state. With them the love of their own soil warms into patriotism, and thus, actuated by the finer feelings of our nature, the humble peasant, on contrasting his northern solitudes with the rich exuberance of the sunny south, may joyfully exclaim with Leyden—

> ' Land of my fathers! though no mangrove here
> O'er thy blue streams her flexile branches rear,
> Nor scaly palm her finger'd scions shoot,
> Nor luscious guava wave her yellow fruit,
> Nor golden apples glimmer from the tree—
> Land of dark heaths and mountains! thou art free.'

# APPENDIX.

### Note A, page 33.

*Halbert's Bog and Milton Bog.*

The Author examined these bogs or marshes in the summer of 1830, and saw them both at that time covered and glistening with water, while the borders of each were fringed all round with thriving reeds and sedges. From the road at the bottom of Brock's-brae, Halbert's Bog extended up to a point in a direct line between New Park farm-house and St. Ninians, while Milton Bog stretched down to where the bridge is erected on the turnpike road, south of the Whins of Milton. Both these swamps were drained by the respective proprietors in the summer of 1842, and the land now is excellent either for the plough or pasturage. Originally they seem to have formed one sheet of water, but a passage in the centre, which was probably narrowest, having been made for the old road leading from Stirling to Kilsyth, the soil washed down by rain from the bank of Brock's-brae, which led up to the Bore-stone, divided at length the one lake into two. If any aquatic plants grew at the bottom of these large pools, they had above five hundred years, calculating from the time of Bruce, for growth and decay; and even if no such roots did grow there, from the natural deposit of ages, the depth of water must have decreased every century. It is not improbable that the hollow may have been used as a reservoir to supply the mills below with water, as the name of Caldam Hill would indicate, and Milton itself might possibly derive its designation from the said mills.

NOTE B, page 45.

*The Bore-stone.*

The current tradition connected with the Bore-stone is, that in its hollow the staff of the royal banner of Scotland stood at the time of the battle of Bannockburn Nimmo, in his "History of Stirlingshire," observes the hole in it was round, about four inches in diameter, and the same in depth. The author saw it in 1830, and the impression on his mind is that the stone might be about sixteen inches in diameter; its colour was blue, and the hole in its centre had been square, each side being about five inches in length and the same in depth, but the edges of the opening were rounded, having been chipped away on every side by a succession of visitors, who intended to preserve the fragments as memorials of the great victory. This mode of destruction seems to have been continued till the relic-hunters were in the habit of going to a smith's shop at the bottom of the bank, the site of which is now levelled for a small-bowling-green, and asking the occupier for the loan of a hammer to break off a bit of the stone to take with them. The process unfortunately was carried on till the stone was broken, and some of the neighbouring inhabitants took away pieces of it for sale. Intimation of this being conveyed to the proprietor of the neighbouring land, he had the spot built round with stone and lime in a square form, about two feet high, and covered over with strong iron grating, fixed into the stones. It will be well if any remains of the original block still occupy the place

The author is inclined to award all due deference to tradition, but in former times it was unusual to fix standard staves in stone in an open field, save in a stationary camp, such as that at the Borough-moor of Edinburgh, where James the Fourth drew his forces together ere they marched southward to Flodden.

In the time of battle the standard, instead of being fixed,

was invariably borne before its owner, but so defended that it could not possibly be taken by the enemy. That of the Bruce at Bannockburn might have its staff placed in the ground ere the struggle began, but it would be raised by man's might, and held aloft, near to Bruce, during the whole of the conflict. Besides, the Bore-stone is nearly half-a-mile from the point where the battle commenced, and its size and socket was far too small and shallow to support the staff of a large standard, streaming and fluttering in the summer breeze.

The author's impression is that the blue stone may have been the base of a small cross, but whether erected before or after 1314, he is unable to say. Crosses were set up on the sides of roads, both in England and Scotland, for various purposes. When the plague devastated a town, the people drew near to a cross, as a place where they could buy and sell without fear of infection. At a funeral, when the way to the place of interment was long, if the bier was set down at any particular spot to afford rest for the mourners, a cross might be reared there, like that below the old churchyard of Ettleton, in Liddesdale, so that travellers in passing might pray for the soul of the departed. Again, in former times, a cross sometimes occupied high ground on the side of a highway, almost within view of a cathedral, to mark the limit of sanctuary, such as Neville's Cross, near Durham. For this purpose there were, in 1144, similar memorials set up near the church of Lesmahago, which David II. granted as a cell to that of Kelso, with this privilege, that—'whoso, for escaping peril of life or limb, flees to the said cell, or comes within the four crosses that stand around it; of reverence to God and St. Machutus, I (the King) grant him my firm peace.'[1] Also, it sometimes occurred that before a battle a cross might be reared where the people, about to be engaged, might supplicate the Almighty for success. Or, if we suppose one to have been

---

[1] *Innes*, p. 197.

placed in the Bore-stone after the battle of Bannockburn was won, what could be more appropriate. on such an occasion, than that every true Scotsman who drew near, then and afterwards, should kneel before it, as the point commanded a full view of the battle-field, and thank God for the deliverance of his beloved country from bondage !

When the body of Robert Bruce was conveyed from Cardross to Dunfermline, had the mourners passed this way and rested the coffin here, it had been well to mark the spot with a memorial of this kind. The author has read of the procession in some work that he cannot now recollect, but he believes the route they followed was not in this direction

On the subject of Crosses see Britton's *Architectural Antiquities of Great Britain,* vol. i. pp. 1-34.

Since writing the above the author chanced to glance into the third volume of Scott's *Border Minstrelsy,* ed 1833, pp 154-5, and his attention was drawn to the following stanzas in Part second of the ballad of 'Thomas the Rhymer.' From what source our great minstrel recovered them we cannot tell, but apparently they are not of his own composition :—

> "The first of blessings I shall thee show,
>   Is by a burn, that's call'd of bread,[1]
> When Saxon men shall tine the bow,
>   And find their arrows lack the head.
>
> ' Beside that brigg, out ower that burn,
>   Where the water bickereth bright and sheen,
> Shall many a falling courser spurn,
>   And knights shall die in battle keen.
>
> ' Beside a headless cross of stone,
>   The libbards there shall lose the gree ;
> The raven shall come, the erne shall go,
>   And drink the Saxon bluid sae free.

---

[1] Bannockburn

"The cross of stone they shall not know,
So thick the corses there shall be."

Sir Charles Lyell, in his *Principles of Geology*, 10th ed. 1867, vol. i. frontispiece, supplies a plate of three massive marble columns in the ruined temple of Jupiter Serapis, at Puzzuoli, in the bay of Baiæ, near Naples. These pillars, having been partly immersed in the sea, indicate very strikingly, by the action of water upon them, how the soil on which they stand has been both depressed and elevated, by volcanic agency, during various periods of time. May the above verses not lead us to something like a retrospect of the same kind? When all evident traces of the battle had become obliterated, and the remains of a cross existed on a spot certainly near to the field of strife, is it not probable that the common people would conclude how those engaged in the conflict must have fallen thickly around the place? Moreover, the writer of the verses, whoever he was, even suppose they were penned by Scott himself, must have been under the impression, whether it might be from his own conviction, or the response of the neighbouring people, that a headless cross was either on or near the field of battle, and if so, where could it stand save in the celebrated Bore-stone? I leave the matter for the candid consideration of those who may wish to institute such an inquiry.

## Note C, p. 122.

*Lists of English who were Slain and taken Prisoners at and after the Battle.*

### No. I.

This record was copied for the author by Mr. George Parker, from the Ashmole MS., 860, fol. 372, *Bodleian Library*, Oxford:—

Nomina occisorum in bello commisso apud Stryvelin,[1] per Scotos, anno 1314, regni regis Edwardi II. 14. fo. 7.

*Barones mortui.*
Gilbertus de Clare, comes Gloucestriæ.
Robertus de Clifford.
Paganus Tybetot.
Willelmus Marescallus.
Ancelmus Mareschall.
Johannes de Mountfort.

*Milites Baneretti mortui.*
Henricus de Bowñ.
Johannes de la Ryver
Edvardus de Maule.
Johannes Comyn.
Robertus de Heestlegh.
Edmundus Comyn
Willelmus Deyncourt.
Egidius de Argenthem.
Johannes Lovell
Edwardus de Hastings.
Robertus Butvyleyn.

Oliuerus de Potton.
Robertus de Lisle
Jacobus de Totorald.
Hugo de Scalys.

*Milites et Nobiles in armis mortui.*
Johannes de Elfeld.
Johannes de Pembrug.
Robertus de Poldesford
Thomas de Vfford.
Reginaldus de Harecourt
Robertus de Applingden.
Thomas de Coudray.
Thomas de Sentleger.
Reginaldus de Ayleby.
Robertus de Bertram miles.
Johannes de Caure.
Milo de Stapleton cum duobus filijs suis.
Walterus de Hakelytelb.

Nomina Valencium nobilium Angliæ capti ibidem apud Stryvelyn, anno 1314, et incarcerati sub custodia Roberti le Bruse regis Scotiæ, anno regni Regis Edvardi II. 14.

Humfridus de Bohun, comes Herefordiæ.
Comes de Anuges.
Willelmus de Latimer.
Johannes Gyffard
Mauricius de Barkele.
Thomas filius suus.
Ingelramus de Humfreville.

Marmaducus de Theynge.
Johannes de Wellington.
Johannes de Claueringe.
Rogerus Tyrell.
Johannes filius suus.
Robertus Maulay.
Henricus filius Hugonis
Thomas de Gray.

---

[1] *i e.*—Bannockburn

## APPENDIX.

Walterus Beauchamp.
Johannes de Willington.
Ricardus de Charons.
Robertus de Fremiñl.[1]
Robertus de Omfravyle.
Johannes de Segrave.
Gilbertus Peche.
Thomas de Ferrers.
Thomas Boutetourt.
Antonius de Lucy.
Bartholomæus de Aynesford.

Richardus Byron.
Walterus de Skydmore.
Johannes Matrevers.
Thomas Thorney.
Rogerus de Sancto Johannes.
Philippus de Courtnay vel Surteney.
Johannes Bluet.
Nicholaus Scot.
Hugo de Hepham.
Edvardus de Hendale.

### No. II.

Scott supplies this list at the end of his notes to *The Lord of the Isles*, but several of the names are incorrectly given, and the following were carefully transcribed from a copy of the continuation of *Trivet's Annals*, in the British Museum :—

From NICHOLAI TRIVETI Annalium Continuatio.
Oxford, 1723.

### LIST OF THE SLAIN.

#### BARONS AND KNIGHTS-BANNERETS

Gilberto de Clare, Com. Glocestriae.
Roberto de Clifford.
Pagano Typetot.
Willielmo le Mareshall.
Joanne Comyn.
Willielmo de Vescey.
Joanne de Monteforti.
Nicolao de Hastelegh.

Willielmo Danycourt.
Ægidis de Argenteym.
Edmundo Comyn.
Joanne Lovel (divite).
Edmundo de Hastynge.
Milone de Stapleton.
Simone Ward.
Roberto de Felton.
Michaele Poinynge.

Edmundo Mauleo.

---

[1] *Sic.*

## KNIGHTS *Slain*

#### SENESCALLO ANGLIAE, BARONIBUS & BANERETTIS, *idem*

Henrico de Boun.
Thoma de Ufford.
Joanne de Elsingfelde.
Joanne de Harecourt.
Waltero de Hakelut.
Philippo de Courtenay.
Hugone de Scales.
Radulpho de Beauchamp

Joanne de Penbrigge, Militibus.

una cum XXXIII. aliis ordinis ejusdem.

## PRISONERS.

#### BARONS AND BARONETS.

Capti quoque & detenti sunt ibidem per Scottos

Dominus Henricus de Boun, Comes Herfordiae.
Comes de Anagos
Dominus Joannes Giffard
Willielmus de Latemer
Mauricius de Bekelegh.
Ingermanus de Umfroynule
Marmaducus de Tewge.
Joannes Wyletone
Robertus de Maulee.
Henricus Filius Hugonis.
Thomas de Gray.
Walterus de Beauchamp.
Richardus de Charonis
Joannes de Wevelmtoun
Robertus de Nevil.
Joannes de Segrave.
Gilbertus Pecche
Joannes de Clavering
Antonius de Lusey.
Radulphus de Canrys.
Joannes de Evere, &

Andreas de Abrembyn.

## KNIGHTS *Prisoners.*

#### BARONES & BANERETTI, MILITES

Insuper subscripti capti & detenti ibidem fuerunt; videlicet :—

Dominus Thomas de Berkeleghe.
Filius Rogeri Tyrel.
Anselmus de Mareschal.
Ægidius de Beauchamp.
Joannes Cyfrewast.
Joannes Bluwet.
Rogerus Corbet.
Gilbertus de Boun.
Bartholomaeus de Enefeld.
Thomas de Ferrars.
Radulphus & Thomas Butetrort.

Joannes & Nicolaus de Keirgestone, fratres.
Willielmus Lovel.
Henricus de Wiletoun.
Baldewinus de Frevile.
Joannes de Clivedone.
(Clindon.)
Adomarus la Souche.

Joannes de Merewode.
Joannes Manfe.
Thomas & Odo Lele, Ercedekene.
Robertus Beaupel, filius.
Joannes Mantravers.
(Mautravers, filius.)
Willielmus & Willielmus Giffard.

Cum aliis XXXIV. ordinis militaris. Et est summa Baronum and Banerettorum una cum Comite Glocestriae ibidem interfectorum XLII. summa vero Comitum Baronum & Banerettorum ibidem captorum & in custodia Scottorum detentorum XXII., Militium quoque LXVIII., Clerici quoque & Scutiferi plures ibidem fuerunt occisi & capti. De quibus & Dominus Rogerus de Northburge, Custos Domini Regis Targiae ab eo ibidem oblatae, una cum Dominus Rogero de Wikenfelde & Thoma de Switone, dicti domini Rogeri Clericis, pariter detinebantur ibidem: ob quod dominus Rex cito postea fieri fecit sigillum, volens illud Privatum Sigillum appellari, ad differentiam Targia sic ut praemittitur ablata. Et est summa totalis tam Comitum Baronum & Banerettorum quam Militum intersectorum & captorum seu detentorum ibidem, una cum tribus Clericis praenominatis, CLIV.—pp. 14-16.

# Biographical Notices

OF THE PRINCIPAL

SCOTTISH AND ENGLISH WARRIORS,

WHO FOUGHT AT

THE BATTLE OF BANNOCKBURN,
A.D. 1314.

# BIOGRAPHICAL NOTICES

THE notices of the following Scottish warriors have been drawn up chiefly from 'Barbour,' 'Kerr,' the 'Peerages' of Scotland, by Crawford and Douglas, and other available sources. For the Arms the author is indebted to 'Nisbet's Heraldry,' Edinburgh, 1816, 2 vols. fol., and 'Laing's Ancient Scottish Seals,' Edinburgh, 1850-66, 2 vols. 4to. Some assistance has also been gleaned from a plate in the first vol. of the 'Acts of the Parliaments of Scotland,' 1844, fol., representing the Seals of the Scottish nobility who signed the celebrated letter to Pope John in 1320.

The memoirs of the English warriors have been derived from Dugdale's 'Baronage,' whence portions of the text were drawn, and from 'The Siege of Carlaverock,' London, 1828, 4to, translated by Sir N. Harris Nicolas, 'The Historic Peerage of England,' 1857, by the same author, 'Hodgson's Northumberland,' with other authorities, among which are the 'Itinerary' and 'Collectanea' of John Leland, which were written and gleaned by that antiquary in the sixteenth century. The shields are supplied from the said 'Siege of Carlaverock,' 'A Roll of Arms' of the reign of Edward the Second, 1829, compared with 'Rolls of Arms' of the reigns of Henry the Third and Edward the Third, 1829, all edited by Nicolas. Boutell's 'Heraldry,' has also thrown light on the subject.

# MEMOIRS OF SCOTTISH WARRIORS.

BRUS OF ANNANDALE.   ARMS OF SCOTLAND.

## Robert the First, King of Scotland.

> Avenger of thy country's shame,
> Restorer of her injured fame,
> Bless'd in thy sceptre and thy sword,
> De Bruce, fair Scotland's rightful Lord,
> Bless'd in thy deeds and in thy fame,
> What lengthened honours wait thy name!
> In distant ages sire to son
> Shall tell thy tale of freedom won,
> And teach his infants in the use
> Of earliest speech to falter Bruce.
>   \*   \*   \*   \*
> Weather and war their rougher trace,
> Have left on that majestic face;
> But 'tis his dignity of eye!
> There, if a suppliant, would I fly,
> Secure 'mid danger, wrongs, and grief,
> Of sympathy, redress, relief—
> That glance, if guilty, would I dread,
> More than the doom that spoke me dead.—SCOTT.

THE many incidents in the life of King Robert Bruce have been narrated most amply by Barbour in his poem of 'The Bruce,' by Kerr in his life of our gallant King, and by Tytler in the first and second volumes of 'The Lives of Scottish Worthies.' Our space is limited, and we can only glance over the great actions of that heroic man, recommending those who desire to know more of him to any or all of these works, wherein they will find nearly all that is known of his history.

Robert de Brus, the grandfather of our hero, married Isabel, daughter of Gilbert de Clare, Earl of Gloucester and Hereford His mother was Isabel, second daughter of David, Earl of Huntingdon, younger brother to William, King of Scots, and succeeding to his father as Lord of Annandale, he, in 1292, was competitor for the crown of Scotland. Dying at Lochmaben in 1295, his son, Robert de Brus, succeeded him in the Lordship of Annandale, and, marrying Margaret, Countess of Carrick, he became Earl of that district by right of his wife. Possessing other estates in England, chiefly in the counties of Durham and Yorkshire, he performed no active part in the affairs of Scotland, and at his death, in 1304, he left to his illustrious son, afterwards King of Scotland, the lands and castle of Lochmaben, together with his possessions in Ayrshire, and resigned also to him the Earldom of Carrick. The great founder of the liberties and independence of his country was born on the 11th July 1274, but whether in the castle of Turnberry, on the Ayrshire coast, or that of Lochmaben, in Dumfriesshire, we are uncertain. Reared amid arms and warriors, he would soon acquire the use of weapons, and when his grandfather and Baliol competed for the crown of Scotland he would be about eighteen years of age. Our hero therefore, from policy, adhered to the interest of England, and in 1296, when Edward the First removed the coronation stone from Scone to Westminster, he made fealty to him at Berwick, and, when about thirty years of age, he received seisin from the English King of the Lordship of Annandale.

After John Baliol was compelled to resign the kingly office to which he had been appointed, his nephew, John Comyn, having sworn fealty to Edward, stood nearest in right of blood to the sceptre of Scotland, and possessing very large estates, he was supported by numerous followers. Robert Bruce, aware of the wretchedness of his native country, is reported to have said to Comyn, 'Support my title to the crown, and I will give you my estate; or give me your estate, and I will support your claim to the

Scottish throne.' Comyn approved of the proposal, an indented document was drawn out thereon, sealed by both parties, and an oath of secrecy taken. It is observed, however, that for his own purpose he acquainted King Edward with the agreement, and Bruce, being at court, on receiving a hint from a friend of his danger, instantly departed for Scotland. No sooner did he reach the castle of Lochmaben than he went to Dumfries, where Comyn resided, and appointing a meeting with him in the convent of the Minorites, they met before the high altar, when Bruce reproached him with his treachery. A quarrel ensuing, Bruce stabbed him with his dagger, and hastened out of the place. His attendants, learning what had occurred, completed the tragedy, and also killed Sir Robert Comyn, who in the scuffle attempted to defend his nephew. This occurred on the 10th February 1305-6.

Robert Bruce had now committed a deed which Edward of England would never pardon. Only two paths were before him: he had either to become a fugitive, or assert his right to the Scottish crown. Accepting as a brave man the latter alternative, he was not without patriotic friends, and in six weeks afterwards he was crowned, at Scone, King of Scotland. In the course of six years from that date he underwent every privation that one in his position could possibly endure, and, to his honour be it said, he neither abated 'heart nor hope' in the prosecution of his design. During that period, out of four of his brothers, three were captured and executed by order of the English King. His queen, a sister, and his daughter, were taken prisoners, and kept in close confinement in England. Yet bravely he surmounted every difficulty, and by his own perseverance, his prudence, and wisdom, his exertions were at last crowned with success on the glorious field of Bannockburn. At this time he would be in the fortieth year of his age.

From his own generous nature, and the ameliorating influence of chivalry which he witnessed in early life, and which, like the spirit of Christianity, brightened up the darker recesses of human existence, he practised all courtesy in dealing with the English after he had made Scotland free. Nor was he slow in following up any advantage he gained if it tended to the security of the land he governed, for, in order to induce England to listen to terms of lasting peace, he harassed that country by successive inroads, enriching thereby his own territory. Desirous also of being reconciled to the Roman See, for he had been greatly traduced to Pope John by the emissaries of England, he induced the nobility of Scotland, in 1320, to draw up a manifesto, which they addressed to the Pontiff, stating in precise but most comprehensive terms the position in which they were placed, and observing that 'so long as a hundred Scotsmen were left alive they would never be subject to the dominion of England. It is not,' they continued, 'for glory, riches, or honour, that we fight, but for that liberty which no good man will consent to lose but with his life.'[1]

After a prosperous period of thirteen years, in the lapse of which Scotland rejoiced in all the benefits she had won, a treaty was at last secured with the sister country, whereby Edward the Third, on the 1st March 1327-8, gave up all claim whatever upon Scotland, and agreed it 'should remain unto Robert King of Scots, and his heirs and successors, free, and divided from England, without any subjection or right of service.' Within a few months afterwards, David, Prince of Scotland, married Joanna, sister to the King of England, so that peace seemed to be secured between both kingdoms. But within two years afterwards, on the 7th June 1329, King Robert died at Cardross, aged fifty-five, in full possession and enjoyment of all that in advanced life tends to our comfort and satisfaction :—

'Honour, love, obedience, troops of friends.'

His remains were interred in the choir, near the high altar, within the church of Dunfermline, and a costly marble tomb made at Paris was shortly afterwards erected over them.

Robert Bruce may, without fear of contradiction, be accounted the greatest monarch that ever occupied the Scottish throne. The talents he possessed by nature, either as a statesman or warrior, were whetted and brought to the keenest edge by the long series of

---

[1] A fac-simile of the original of this important Declaration is given in the 'Acts of Parliament of Scotland,' fol. 1844, vol. i. facing p. 115, illustrated with representations of the seals of the several noblemen. A translation is printed in the collection of tracts entitled 'Miscellanea Scotica,' vol. iii p. 123 Another copy appears in the 'Harleian Miscellany,' vol. i p 128, 8vo ed , 12 vols , Lond. 1808

privations he endured, till the time came when he was enabled to turn them to glorious account. Even when surrounded by the pomp of royalty, and executing his kingly duties with promptitude, prudence, and wisdom, he never overlooked the poor of his realm, and was kind and generous to all around him. There could be no finer or more gentle trait than he showed to the poor washerwoman overtaken by the pains of labour in Ireland, when he stayed on her account his whole army, as it was about to march to the north. Barbour describes the circumstance very beautifully.[2]

The compiler has often revolved in his mind the personal appearance of Bruce, being desirous to ascertain whether his complexion was dark or fair, and his stature high or low. The following single sentence from 'Historia Majoris Britanniae,' ed. Edin. 1740, p. 194, may afford pleasure to those interested in such an inquiry :—

'Erat enim pulchro, decoro & vegete corpore, latis humeris, venusta facie, flava more borealium caesarie, caeruleis & micantibus oculis, ingenio promptus, & ad dicendum vernacula in lingua orator acer & omnibus pergratus.'

We have no cause to doubt the accuracy of this description of the great Scottish king. The fair or yellow hair is indicative of the sanguine temperament, and we know that Bruce was remarkable for energy both of body and mind. His strength was also evinced in the numerous encounters he had with the English at and previous to the battle of Bannockburn. His descendants, the Stewards, though lacking his moral and intellectual power, inherited, so far as we can discover, some traces of the features and complexion of their illustrious ancestor.

Of the physical proportions of Bruce we have proof, from his grave being discovered, 17th February 1818, and opened in the presence of the chief officers of Scotland on the 5th November in the following year. The marble tomb which had been placed over it was entirely gone, but the skeleton was laid bare. The shoulders had been strong and broad, and the whole length, from the sole of the foot to the top of the cranium, was five feet eleven inches, therefore he had been about six feet high. A cast was taken from

[2] Page 320.

the skull, which is still preserved. There were four or five teeth wanting in the upper jaw, with a considerable fracture of the same in front, which had evidently been caused by a blow received, it is thought, in one of the encounters to which he was exposed in early life [3]

In Hearne's edition of 'Fordun,' quoted by Tytler, vol. 1. p. 393, we have the following translation into Scottish rhyme of seven leonine Latin verses, constituting what is called 'King Robert's testament.' We give Tytler's copy, which contains one line more than that of Ridpath, p 290 —

'On fut suld be all Scottis weire,
Be hyll and moss thaimself to weire,
Lat wod for wallis be ; bow, and spier,
And battle-axe, their fechting gear.
That ennymeis do thaim na dreire,
In strait placis gar keip all stoire,
And birnen the planen land thaim befoire,
Thanen sall they pass away in haist
Quhen that thai find nathing bot waist ;
With wylles and wakenen of the nycht
And mekil noyse maid on hycht ;
Thanen shall thai turnen with gret affrai
As thai were chasit with swerd away
This is the counsall and intent
Of gud King Robert's testament.'

Bruce married first, Isabella, daughter of Donald, tenth Earl of Mar, by whom he had a daughter Marjory, who, in 1315, married Walter, the Steward of Scotland, but she died in the following year, leaving a son, who was afterwards King Robert the Second ; secondly, in 1302, Bruce took to wife Elizabeth, eldest daughter of Richard de Burgh,[4] second Earl of Ulster, in Ireland, by whom he had one son, who, on the death of his father, became King David the Second, but he died childless in the forty-seventh year of his age. King Robert had also, by the said Elizabeth, two daughters, Margaret and Matilda. The said Margaret married William, Earl of Sutherland, by whom she had two sons, John and William. John died at Lincoln in 1361, and William carried on

---

[3] See *Archæologia Scotica*, vol. ii. pp. 435-50.
[4] Crawfurd calls her Mary, daughter of Ailmer de Burc, p 72

the line of the Sutherland family, which, after the commencement of the present century, was represented by the Marchioness of Stafford, Countess of Sutherland in her own right. Matilda, the other daughter, married a private gentleman, who, according to Fordun, was named Thomas Isaac.—See *Kerr*, vol. ii. pp. 481-2.

> ARMS.—Paternal shield when Brus of Annandale—Or, a saltire and chief gules. On being crowned, Bruce assumed the arms of Scotland—Or, a lion rampant gules, armed and langued azure, within a double tressure, flowered and counter-flowered of the second.

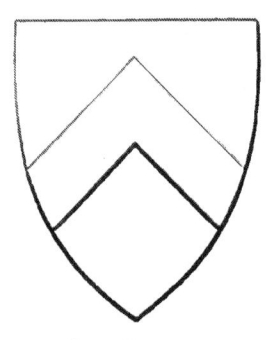

## Sir Edward Bruce.

SIR EDWARD BRUCE, brother to the king, was next to him in age, and performed an important part in the early history of Scotland. After the coronation of Bruce in 1306, he resigned to Sir Edward the Earldom of Carrick, with the title and dignity thereof, but, in default of heirs, the said earldom, with its honours, was to revert to the crown. Sir Edward was present at the enterprise against Perth soon afterwards, and on the failure of that attempt, he remained with his illustrious brother for a time, sharing in all his privations. But in 1308, when the fortune of his family seemed in the ascendant, he invaded Galloway, and with his usual energy attacked near Cree and defeated Sir Ingram de Umfreville and Sir John de Saint John, who commanded the inhabitants of that district for the King of England. Afterwards Sir John de Saint John repaired to England, and collecting a large body of horsemen, he again advanced into Galloway, intending to circumvent and cut off Edward Bruce, but the latter, receiving accurate intelligence of his movements, arranged his troops, and bore down on the English so suddenly, that he put them to utter confusion, and on a second furious charge they were entirely overcome and put to flight. From the success of Sir Edward Bruce in this skirmish, he proceeded onward, everywhere reducing the people to obedience, and bringing them under the allegiance of his royal brother. About this time, it is probable that, being already the sixth Earl of Carrick, Sir Edward, for his gallant conduct, was made Lord of Galloway, which title he held till the time of his death.

He next comes prominently before us at the siege of Stirling Castle, where, his bravery being of slender avail, he agreed with the Governor thereof, Sir Philip Mowbray, for a protracted surrender of the fortress. Here he displayed great lack of prudence, and the result was the battle of Bannockburn, in which, to his credit be it said, his bravery in war was most conspicuous. At length, when Scotland was rescued from thraldom, he went in pursuit of the Earl of Hereford, who, with a number of followers, had taken refuge in Bothwell Castle, and speedily forced them to surrender. In union with Sir James Douglas, he next led an army into England, penetrating as far as Richmondshire, and returned to his own country laden with spoil.

Nearly two years after the battle of Bannockburn, the Irish chiefs of the province of Ulster were much dissatisfied with the English government of that country, and knowing how the Scots had successfully secured their national independence, they implored Robert Bruce to aid them in regaining their freedom, offering to accept his brother Edward as their king. Sir Edward Bruce, who had no scope for his martial energy in peace, probably considered it was no difficult matter to expel the English from that kingdom, and occupy the throne himself. King Robert would appear to have assisted him in the design, for a great many of the nobility of Scotland accompanied Sir Edward in the expedition, which took place during May 1315. After undergoing various changes of fortune, and overcoming many obstacles, Sir Edward Bruce was crowned king of Ireland about a year after he effected a landing in that country. But his high position afforded him no relief from enemies at home and abroad, and he was slain at the battle of Dundalk, in October 1318. In the previous year, a dispensation was granted by the Pope, at Avignon, permitting him to marry Isabella, daughter to William, Earl of Ros, for they were within the third and fourth degrees of consanguinity, but he left no legitimate issue. Three natural sons—Robert, Alexander, and Thomas—survived him, who became successively Earls of Carrick.

ARMS.—The old Earls of Carrick bore, Argent, a cheveron gules.

## Thomas Randolph, Earl of Moray.

> For and men spek off him trewly;
> He wes swa curageous ane knycht,
> Sa wyss, sa worthy, and sa wycht,
> And off sa souerane gret bounté
> That mekill off him may spokyn be.
> BARBOUR.

THOMAS RANDOLPH of Strathdon succeeded his father of the same name, who was Sheriff of Roxburgh in 1266. His mother was Lady Isabel Bruce, eldest sister to King Robert. His first appearance in public life was at the coronation of his uncle at Scone, in March 1306. Espousing the royal cause, he was taken prisoner by the English at Methven, and, through the intercession of Adam de Gordon, obtained mercy, being admitted to swear fealty to Edward the First. Again, in 1308, he was captured on Line Water, in Tweeddale, by James Douglas; and having in his defence spoken rudely to King Robert, he was ordered to close confinement; but being afterwards received into favour, he distinguished himself in 1312 by taking the castle of Edinburgh by escalade, he himself being the third assailant who mounted the ladder. It is supposed that soon after this time he obtained the charter of his honour, for, in the Parliament of 1315, he appears under the title of the Earl of Moray.

We have observed what trust was placed upon him by Robert Bruce previous to and during the battle of Bannockburn, and how well he performed his duty on that eventful day. When the settlement of the crown of Scotland was made in 1315, it was enacted that should the heir be in minority, Thomas Randolph would be his or her guardian, and also Regent of the kingdom. After the death in Ireland of Edward Bruce, a second enactment was completed in 1318, whereby the heir to the crown, if under age, was to be placed under the tutorage of the Earl of Moray, who was also to be Guardian of Scotland, and failing him these offices were to devolve on Lord James Douglas. During 1319, Randolph, in conjunction with Sir James Douglas, commanded the army that invaded England, whereby victory was secured to the Scots near Boroughbridge, in Yorkshire. In the following year his name appears second on the list of those patriots who signed the remarkable letter to Pope John, wherein the independence of Scotland was so emphatically maintained, and which assisted afterwards in producing the happiest results.

In 1323 he went on an embassy to the Pope, waited upon his Holiness at Avignon, and, according to Hailes, with the most consummate ability elicited from him an acknowledgment of the title of king to Robert Bruce. Two years afterwards he was sent ambassador to Charles le Bel, King of France, when he completed an alliance, offensive and defensive, between that kingdom and Scotland. About midsummer, in 1327, he and Douglas again led an army into the Bishopric of Durham, where they foiled the youthful Edward the Third, and returned with much booty into their own land.

When Robert Bruce died in 1329, the Earl of Moray became Regent of Scotland, and undertook the office of guardian to David the Second, discharging these duties with most exemplary fidelity, and, by his strict administration of justice, securing everywhere peace and prosperity to the people. But about three years afterwards, when the English were preparing to invade Scotland, the Regent Moray raised an army, and, though afflicted with severe pain from a confirmed stone disease, he exerted himself greatly, and died on the march, at Musselburgh, on the 20th July 1332. Some of our annalists observe he died of poison, administered by his chaplain, an English friar, through design of Edward the Third, but Lord Hailes contradicts the assertion. Barbour, however, puts upon record he was 'pusonit,' and Scott inclines to the opinion that the beautiful ballad of *Lord Randal* had its origin from that tradition.

Of the external appearance of Randolph, we learn from the pen of Barbour that he bore some resemblance to his uncle Robert Bruce. These are his lines :—

> ' I will discryve now his fassoun
> And part off his condicioun.
> He wes off mesurabill statur,
> And weile porturat at mesur ;
> With braid wesage, plesand and fayr,
> Curtaiss at poynt, and debonayr ;
> And off rycht sekyr contenyng.
> Lawté he lowyt atour all thing ;
> Falset, tresoun, and felony
> He stud agayne ay encrely.
> He heyit honour ay, and larges,
> And ay mantemyt rychtwysnes.'—P. 197.

Randolph, Earl of Moray, married Isabel, only daughter of Sir John Stewart of Bonkyl, by whom he got the barony of Garlies. He had two sons—Thomas, second Earl, and John, third Earl of Moray—both of whom died childless, and one daughter, Lady Agnes, who was married to Patrick, ninth Earl of Dunbar and March, who in her right became possessed of the earldom of Moray.

ARMS.—Argent, three cushions pendent by the corners, within a double tressure, flowered and counter-flowered with fleurs-de-lis gules. The double tressure was added from Randolph being a son to the sister of King Robert Bruce.

## Sir James Douglas.

> He wes in all his dedis lele;
> For him dedeynyeit nocht to dele
> With trechery, na with falset.
> His hart on hey honour wes set:
> And hym contenyt on sic maner,
> That all him luffyt that war him ner.—BARBOUR.

JAMES DOUGLAS was son to William Douglas, who, on the usurpation by Edward the First of the dominion of Scotland, withstood the tyrant, and being imprisoned, he died at York about 1302. His estates being forfeited, Edward had bestowed them on Lord Clifford; and James Douglas, a young man, being left almost destitute, went to France, and, probably by the assistance of friends, lived at Paris nearly three years. On the year after that of his father's decease, he returned to Scotland, and on presenting himself before William Lamberton, Bishop of St. Andrews, the good prelate received him with great kindness. The last time that Edward the First overran Scotland, he called together a meeting of the barons at Stirling, and Lamberton, having attended the summons, took with him the youthful Douglas. Watching an opportunity, he presented Douglas to the monarch as a squire who claimed to be admitted to his service, and asked that he would be pleased to restore him his inheritance. This was denied, and Douglas thereupon waited an opportunity whereby he might be enabled to lend his aid to the benefit of his country.

This was not long in presenting itself, for when Bruce had slain Comyn at Dumfries, and laid claim to the crown of Scotland, Douglas asked the bishop for leave to join his party. He obtained secret encouragement both by a horse which he was to secure against the will of Lamberton's servant, and by money, wherewith he was quietly supplied. He met Bruce at Erickstone, near the head of Clydesdale, who was journeying from Lochmaben to Glasgow, and the latter gave him open welcome. He was entrusted with the command of a party of men, and the Bruce soon found by his excellent qualities that he had secured an able supporter, who proved himself deserving of all confidence and honour. In the skirmishes and warfare which followed, Douglas repeatedly took from the English his paternal castle of Douglas, cutting off the garrison, and on the Borders he regained the forests of Ettrick and Jedburgh to the sway of Bruce.

Afterwards, on the water of Line, he took prisoners Stewart of Bonkyl and Thomas Randolph, who were in the service of England, and led them to the king, whom he assisted greatly in the invasion of Lorn, and in defeating the chief of that name, at the base of Cruachan Ben. His next great exploit was the capture of Roxburgh Castle, in 1312, when the English, who had possession of that fortress, were regaling themselves on the eve of Lent. At Bannockburn, he and the young Steward lent their aid in securing victory to the Scots, and after the battle he pursued the monarch of England, chasing him till the castle of Dunbar gave shelter to the fugitive king.

In 1316, when Bruce was assisting his brother Edward in his unfortunate attempt to maintain his position as king of Ireland, to Douglas was committed the charge of defending the eastern borders. The Earl of Arundel, being aware of the absence of Bruce, and knowing the prowess of Douglas, raised a large army to overpower him, but the latter, learning by spies of the approach of his enemy, drew him into an ambush in the valley of the Jed, and he was defeated. On this occasion Douglas, it is said, slew Thomas de Richmont with his own hand.[1] Many other daring and gallant actions he performed, the details of which our space forbids us to enumerate.

For several years Douglas assisted in leading the martial men of Scotland into England, and wasting and plundering the northern counties. On the last of these occasions, Edward the Third, then a stripling, opposed Douglas and Randolph, but he had no chance whatever in circumventing or beating back these tried and intrepid warriors. When at last Robert Bruce lay in expectation of death, he called Douglas and asked him to undertake the charge of carrying his heart to Palestine, that it might be interred in the Holy Sepulchre of Jerusalem, to which he readily agreed. Embalming the relic, and enclosing it in a silver case, he hung it by a chain around his neck, and embarking with a goodly company at Berwick, he set sail, and on his track visited Alphonsus, the youthful king of Leon and Castile, who at that time was at war with Osmyn, the Moorish commander of Granada. Our brave knight joined the Christians at once, and in a desperate encounter, detaching the casket containing the heart of Bruce, he threw it before him among the Moors, saying, 'Pass onward as thou wert wont, and Douglas will follow thee or die!'[2] In the violent onset he was slain, after which his mournful companions found his body, and the casket, which they conveyed home. The heart, by order of Randolph, was deposited in Melrose Abbey, and the bones of the hero were carefully entombed in the church at Douglas, among those of his forefathers.

---

[1] "Richmont, who commanded under the Earl of Arundel, entered the forest of Jedworth with ten thousand Englishmen, provided with axes to cut down the trees, and attack Sir James Douglas, to whom the defence of the march had been entrusted; but that cautious leader having constructed for himself and his followers a camp at Lintalee, a short distance above Jedburgh, issued thence, and giving battle to Richmont, killed him and routed his army."—*White's Battle of Otterburn*, p. 16.

[2] This recalls to our thoughts all the desperate struggles he had encountered with Bruce, and is indeed highly poetical—more so indeed than Nelson's signal at the last of his battles:—'England expects every man to do his duty!'

## SIR JAMES DOUGLAS.

According to Fordun, Sir James Douglas engaged seventy times in battle. Of these he was beaten in thirteen several encounters, and in the other fifty-seven he came off victorious. All his life he contrived, like Wallace, to defend his face from any scar; and this astonished the Spaniards when they saw him, and knew in what struggles he had been engaged. We have a striking picture of him in Barbour, who undoubtedly had the information from those who had seen him. The slight lisp in his speech is remarkably characteristic:—

> 'Bot he wes nocht so fayr, that we
> Suld spek gretly off his beauté.
> In wysage wes he sumdeill gray,
> And had blak har, as Ic hard say;
> But off lymmys he wes weill maid,
> With banys gret and schuldrys braid;
> His body wes wey'll [maid and lenye;]
> As thai that saw hym said to me.
> Quhen he wes blyth, he wes lufly,
> And meyk and sweyt in cumpany,
> Bot quha in battaill mycht him se,
> All othir contenance had he.
> And in spek wlispyt he sum deill:
> Bot that sat him rycht wondre weill.'—Pp. 14-5.

Sir James Douglas died unmarried, and had two natural sons, Sir William Douglas, called the 'The Knight of Liddesdale,' and Archibald, who was made prisoner at Halidon Hill in 1333. Sir James was succeeded in the Lordship of Douglas by his brother Hugh, and his youngest brother, Archibald Douglas, was made Lord of Galloway, and afterwards came to be Governor of Scotland.

ARMS.—The old arms of the family, before Douglas became a surname, were, Argent, on a chief azure, three mullets of the field. But Sir James, on being commissioned by Bruce to carry his heart to Palestine, bore on his shield, Argent a man's heart gules, ensigned with an imperial crown proper, on a chief azure, three stars of the first.

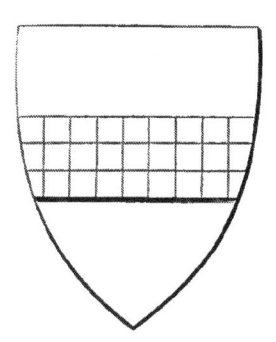

## Walter, the High Steward of Scotland.

WALTER, the High Steward of Scotland, was born in 1293, and succeeding his father James in 1309, he brought a gallant body of men to assist King Robert Bruce immediately before the battle of Bannockburn. Along with his kinsman Sir James Douglas, as has been observed, he was appointed leader of one of the divisions of the Scottish army, and proved himself worthy of that honour. Towards the close of 1314, when the illustrious Scottish prisoners were to be returned from England, he was engaged to receive them on the borders, and, accordingly, he took under his charge Elizabeth, wife of King Robert, the King's daughter Marjory, his sister Christian, the young Earl of Mar, and Robert, Bishop of Glasgow. It is probable he thereby formed an attachment to the Princess Marjory, for they were married in the following year. The union, however, was destined to be of short duration, for Lady Marjory died in 1316, leaving an only son, Robert, who afterwards became king. In that year, when Bruce passed over to Ireland to assist his brother Edward, king of that country, Walter the Steward and Sir James Douglas were appointed governors of Scotland. In 1318, when Berwick was recovered from the English, that town was committed to the charge of the Steward, who made every preparation for its safety, and in the following year he defended it against the King of England and a royal army, who were beaten off and compelled to abandon the siege. His name next appears among those of the patriotic nobles and barons of Scotland on the famous letter to Pope John, written in 1320. Next year he acquired a grant of the lands of Eckford, in Roxburghshire, Methven in Perthshire, and Kellie in the county of Forfar, forfeited by Roger Mowbray; also, with the exception of the valley of Liddel, he got the lands of Nisbet, the baronies of Langnewton, Maxton, and Caverton in Roxburghshire, which had belonged to William Lord Soulis, the Seneschal of Scotland. Again, in 1322, the Steward, with Douglas and Randolph, by a forced march, attempted to surprise Edward the Second at Biland Abbey, in Yorkshire; but the king escaped with difficulty to York, and the pursuers, with five hundred horsemen, waited till evening at the gates of that city, that the English might come forth and give them battle. In this way, serving his king and country so long as he was able to perform such duty, he died on the 9th April 1326, aged 33 years.

Walter the Steward married, first, Alice, second daughter of Sir John Erskine, by whom he had one daughter. Secondly, in 1315, he led to the altar the Princess Marjory, whose son became High Steward, till he occupied the throne as Robert the Second. Thirdly, he married Isabel, sister of Sir John Graham of Abercorn, by whom he had a son and daughter.

ARMS.—Or, a fesse cheque azure and argent.

# MEMOIRS OF ENGLISH WARRIORS.

### King Edward the Second.

KING EDWARD THE SECOND was one of six brothers, sons of Edward the First, but three died in the lifetime of their father, and he, being the eldest living in 1307, ascended the throne in the twenty-third year of his age. Though of an affectionate and kindly disposition, he loved pleasure and worldly comfort, and was apt to leave state affairs to be transacted by his youthful favourites, rather than call together his nobility, and avail himself of their deliberation in arranging the more important matters of his kingdom. From this cause arose nearly all his misfortunes; and not alone did he endure the evils consequent on his inability, but the whole people of England, high and low, suffered less or more under his sway.

His first favourite was Piers de Gaveston, son to a gentleman of Guienne. They had been companions from boyhood, and the latter had considerable ability, was ready-witted, and in some tournaments he was enabled by his address to unhorse several Earls of England. Edward the First, perceiving the ascendency towards evil that Piers had gained over his son, caused him to be banished from the realm, and afterwards exacted from his son an oath that the dissolute youth should never be permitted to return to England.

## KING EDWARD THE SECOND. 171

No sooner, however, had the father died than Gaveston was recalled, and loaded with honours and rewards, to the displeasure and enmity of the whole of the English nobility. Assaults and aggravation continued on both sides for the space of five years, till Gaveston, being chased as a fugitive, fell into the hands of the Earl of Warwick, who caused him to be beheaded on a hill at a short distance north from that county town. A wood now crowns the eminence, but the spot of execution is marked by an obelisk of a gray colour, which points upward from among the neighbouring trees.

On his other favourites, the Spensers, it is unnecessary here to enlarge. One of them accompanied him to Bannockburn; and here King Edward's lack of foresight and judgment has been plainly shown, previous to and at the battle, from the circumstance of causing his army to march towards Bruce as if he had been going to celebrate a marriage festival, instead of encountering the chances of war, and neither he nor his nobles provided any means of safety for the English forces in the event of a defeat. At the time of the battle, it may be observed, he was about thirty years of age.

Many serious quarrels arose between Edward and the chief men of his realm, which occasioned much bloodshed. This continued for the space of twelve years, for the nobility envied and hated Spenser, till at last they first brought destruction on the father of the object of their resentment, and afterwards upon himself. The wealth heaped on these favourites of royalty was enormous, the details of which are to be found in our historical authorities. Besides these evils, the Scots, under Bruce, Randolph, and Douglas, by frequent expeditions over the Border, caused much loss and suffering to the inhabitants of the northern counties. Rebellions were continued against the king, part of which he suppressed, but ultimately he was wounded in his tenderest feelings by one who ought to have proved through life his most faithful stay. His queen, named Isabella, was a daughter of Philip le Bel, King of France. She was a beautiful, but an unprincipled woman. She bore him two sons and two daughters, and afterwards went to her relatives in France, where she plotted against him. An improper intimacy had sprung up between her and a rebel and exile, Roger Mortimer of Wigmore, so that when her lord and husband had become unpopular in England, she brought, with her paramour, a force over to this country, and by aid from the chief adherents of her designs, Edward was captured and imprisoned for a considerable period. He suffered much indignity, and by the wicked machinations of his enemies he was most cruelly put to death in Berkeley Castle, on the night of the 21st September 1327.

> ARMS.—The Royal shield bore, Gules, three leopards or lions passant guardant, in pale, or. The same insignia were borne by the king's father and grandfather, and he had them embroidered on his surcoat, and the caparisons of his horse. Le Roy de Engletere, porte de goules, a iij lupars passauns de or.—*Roll of Arms.*

### Gilbert de Clare, Earl of Gloucester.

GILBERT DE CLARE was nephew to the king, his father of the same name having married Joan of Acre, daughter of Edward the First. He was born in 1290, so that, at the battle of Bannockburn, he would be about twenty-four years of age. After the death of his father, his mother Joan having married a squire, Ralph de Monthermer, who used the title of her first husband, yet her son Gilbert in the first year of Edward the Second, being in the wars of Scotland, is acknowledged by our historians as Earl of Gloucester, and though only in his eighteenth year, he had livery of his lands, the king having satisfaction that he was under age. Again, in the second year of the king's reign, he was captain-general of the nobles who were in his retinue, and in the year following he had several manors given him for life, in case he had no issue. Next year, 1311, he was appointed Guardian of the whole realm of England, while the king was absent in Scotland. Moreover, before the battle of Bannockburn he was sent as one of the king's ambassadors to France to treat and conclude on certain articles of peace between both realms. On his return he accompanied the king to Scotland; and being captain of the vanguard at the battle of Bannockburn, he was slain, whereupon Bruce sent his body to King Edward at Berwick, to be interred where the latter should determine. Stow tells us his remains were buried at Tewksbury.

He married Maude, daughter of John de Burgh, son of Richard Earl of Ulster, and left no children, since John his son died in his lifetime. In expectation of issue, a considerable time was allowed to the said Maude, and, ultimately, his large inheritance was shared by his three sisters—Alianore, who married first, Hugh le Despencer, and secondly, William Lord Zouch of Mortimer; Margaret, wife first of Piers Gaveston, and secondly of Hugh de Audley; and Elizabeth, married first to John de Burgh, secondly to Theobald de Verdon, and thirdly to Roger D'Amorie. The lady last mentioned, to her honour be it said, was the foundress of the College of Clare Hall in Cambridge.

ARMS.—Or, three chevronels gules.
De or, a iij cheverons de goules.—*Roll of Arms.*

A drawing of this shield, whence the cut is designed, was kindly procured by the engraver, Mr. John Cleghorn, from a Roll of Arms of the English nobility who were present at a tournament held at Stepney, 28th February 1308, in Cole's MSS. vol. 47, p. 145, deposited in the British Museum.

Sir Giles d'Argentine was a hero of romance in real life.—HAILES.

## Sir Giles de Argentine.

THIS warrior belonged to a family remarkable for bravery, who possessed lands in the counties of Cambridge, Norfolk, Suffolk, and Hertford. In 1193 Reginald de Argentine was sheriff for the counties of Cambridge and Huntington, and, four years afterward, entered into the like office for the counties of Essex and Hertford. Again, his son in 1223 was sheriff for the counties of Essex and Hertford, and was made Governor of Hertford Castle. Also, he became sheriff for the counties of Cambridge and Huntington, and in 1226 was one of the stewards for the king's household. This noble knight, of great prowess, went in 1229 on a pilgrimage to the Holy Land, but departed this life in 1246. Another of the family of the same name, being a Knight Templar, was standard-bearer of the Christian army; and in a great battle in 1237 against the Turks, near Antioch, in Palestine, he bore the banner till his legs and arms were both broken, and there he was slain.

Sir Giles de Argentine, another knight of great valour, and son to him who died in 1246, was constituted Governor of Windsor

Castle in 1263. Joining, however, the rebellious barons after the battle of Lewes, in company with his son, he was elected one of nine counsellors to assume the government of the realm. But the insurrection being suppressed at the battle of Evesham, his lands were sequestrated. At his death, which occurred in 1282, he was seised of a certain manor lying in Weldburne, also of the manor of Great Wymondeley, in the county of Cambridge, which he held by grand Sergeantie, *namely*, 'to serve the king on the day of his coronation with a silver cup.' His son and heir, Reginald, was under age, but soon after his father's death, doing homage, he had livery of his lands in the counties of Cambridge, Norfolk, Suffolk, and Hertford. He was summoned as a baron to Parliament in 1297, but, dying in 1307, he was succeeded by John de Argentine, the second baron, who died about 1318.

The manor of Wimley or Wymondeley is said to have come into possession of the Argentines by marriage with the heiress of Fitz Tees, who was descended from David de Argentine, a Norman who came over with William the Conqueror. The male line ceased with John de Argentine, the fifth baron, and the manor was carried by his only daughter into the house of Allington, on her marriage with William Allington, an ancestor of the family.

Of this line came the subject of our notice, Sir Giles de Argentine, but in what degree he stood we are uncertain. He was well known to Bruce in the court of England before 1306, and our archives afford us a glance into the military prowess of the man at the tournament already mentioned, which was held at Stepney, in which he attained, in the struggle for skill and strength, among the nobility of England the chief post of renown. In pursuit of the honourable profession of arms, he seems to have gone abroad, and in the wars of Palestine he encountered the Saracens on three several occasions, when in each conflict he slew two of their chief warriors. He also entered the service of **Henry VII.** of Luxenburgh, Emperor of Germany, and following the brief but brilliant career of that illustrious individual, he acquired such fame as to be accounted one of the bravest warriors of his time. In common estimation the said Emperor Henry occupied the highest point of honour, Robert, King of Scotland, the second, and De Argentine maintained the third place. In 1313

## 176 BIOGRAPHICAL NOTICES.

he would appear to have returned to England, and from his acknowledged merit was appointed to remain by the side of King Edward on the field of Bannockburn. All our historians agree in extolling his bravery, and his loss was everywhere lamented. Bruce, from the intimacy which once subsisted between them, took especial care of his body, causing it to be buried in St. Patrick's Church, near Edinburgh.—*Bellenden, Hailes, Kerr, etc.*

ARMS.—The bearings of De Argentine, as we learn from the Roll of Arms already alluded to in Cole's MSS., were, Gules, three covered cups between nine crosses crosslet argent.

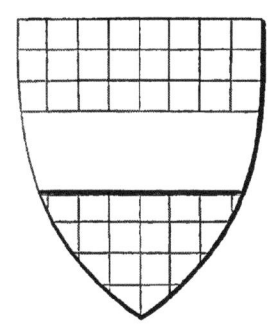

### Robert Clifford.

ROBERT DE CLIFFORD, a noted warrior in the time of Edward the First, was born about Easter in 1274. When near his thirteenth year he succeeded his grandfather in his baronial honours. Dugdale says he was at the battle of Dunbar in 1296. During the year following, in May, he was summoned to attend the king with horse and arms in an expedition beyond sea, and afterwards he was sent from Carlisle with an hundred men-at-arms and twenty thousand foot, to plunder the Scots, which he accomplished; and, after great slaughter, he returned to England with much booty. Forthwith he was appointed Justice of all the king's forests beyond Trent, and on the following year he was made Governor of

## ROBERT CLIFFORD. 177

Nottingham Castle. Again, in 1298-9, being constituted King's Lieutenant and Captain-General in the Counties of Cumberland, Westmorland, and Lancaster, and over Annandale and the Marches of Scotland, he was joined in commission with the Bishop of Durham and others to consider how the castles in England could be garrisoned, and how the Marches might be defended. Soon after, he was summoned to the Scottish wars, and received his first writ to Parliament at the close of 1299.

Thus, in his twenty-fifth year, he was honoured with his sovereign's confidence, and was present with him, in 1300, at the siege of Carlaverock Castle.[1] Here Clifford especially distinguished himself, for he served in the third squadron, and was led by the king in person. As a reward for his bravery he was appointed Governor of the castle when it surrendered, and his banner was placed on its battlements. On the year previous to the death of Edward the First, for his numerous services he had a grant of the borough of Hartlepool, and of the lands of Robert de Brus. He was also sent with Aymer de Valence against the said Robert, and, moreover, had a grant of the lands of Christopher de Seyton. At the death-bed of the king in 1307, he heard the monarch's orders to prevent the return of Gaveston to England. Under Edward the Second he was again Governor of Nottingham Castle, and was appointed Earl-Marshal of England. Soon after the wardenship of the Marches of Scotland devolved upon him, and he became Governor of that kingdom. Several additional grants of lands were also made to him in recompense of his services, and in 1313 he had an acquittance from the king for the jewels, horses, etc., which had belonged to Piers de Gaveston, for he adhered to the Earl of Lancaster against the royal favourite, and obtained pardon from the king for the active part he took in causing his death. He was regularly summoned to Parliament from 1299 to 1313, and fell, as has been stated, at Bannockburn, in the forty-first

---

[1] The French poem on this occasion, written it is supposed by Walter of Exeter, a Franciscan Friar, has excited great interest among heralds and historians. It was edited, as already stated, by Sir N. Harris Nicolas, and from the memoirs of the warriors in the volume the compiler has drawn much condensed information.

year of his age. His defeat by Randolph on the day previous to the battle may have led him to rush more unguardedly on the Scottish spears. His body is said to have been interred at Shap Abbey, in Westmoreland.

Clifford married Maude, daughter and ultimately co-heir of Thomas de Clare, Steward of Waltham Forest, son of Thomas, youngest son of Richard de Clare, Earl of Gloucester and Hertford. By her he had issue Roger, who, at fifteen years of age, succeeded him in the barony. Another son was Robert, from whom descended the baronial line of Clifford, which, in the time of Henry the Eighth, was raised to the Earldom of Cumberland. Some authorities say he had other two sons, John and Andrew, and a daughter, Idunea, the wife of Henry, Lord Clifford.

ARMS.—Checky or, and azure, a fess gules. *Checkere de or e de azure, a une fesse de goules.*—*Roll of Arms.*

### Aymer de Valence, Earl of Pembroke.

THIS distinguished man was born about 1280, being the third son of William de Valence, who was created Earl of Pembroke by his uterine brother King Henry the Third. About the sixteenth year of his age, he succeeded his father in his honours—two elder brothers having previously died without issue. He was tall in stature, and of a sallow complexion, whence Piers Gaveston bestowed on him the *sobriquet* of 'Joseph the Jew.' The earliest notice of him on record is, that in 1297 he was summoned to Parliament as a baron, though it is said he was entitled to the Earldom of Pembroke; yet that title was not bestowed on him in public records till 1307. It is, however, clear that from the decease of his father he ranked above all barons save Henry of Lancaster, who, being of royal blood, is mentioned next to Earls. About his eighteenth year he was sent by the king as an ambassador, to treat of a truce between England and France; and in the three following years he was in the Scottish wars, and accompanied the king in 1300 to the siege of Carlaverock. He was again in the wars of Scotland about 1302, and got permission to leave the realm on his own affairs. In 1305 the castles of Selkirk and Traquair, and the borough of Peebles, with other possessions in that kingdom, were granted to him to hold by the service of one knight's fee, and shortly afterward he was constituted Guardian of the Marches of Scotland towards Berwick, besides being entrusted with the sole command of the English forces which were levied against Bruce.

It has been mentioned that in the discharge of his office as leader of the English troops he established his headquarters at Perth, and after Bruce had been crowned, in attempting to reduce that town he was attacked suddenly by De Valence, and suffered a serious defeat. In the following year, however, Bruce met him by appointment, near Loudon Hill, and with a small body of spearmen, succeeded in vanquishing his squadrons of mounted horsemen so effectually that they fled in the utmost confusion to Bothwell. Again, De Valence was present at the death of King Edward the First, and, with other noblemen, received the monarch's injunctions to afford his son their support and counsel, so as to prevent the return of Gaveston to England. Being summoned to Parliament by his proper title, Earl of Pembroke, he was present at the coronation of Edward the Second, and carried the youthful king's left boot, the spur belonging to it being borne by the Earl of Cornwall. In the same year, he was sent with Otho de Grandison and others to the Pope on special business, and on the decease of his mother, by doing homage, he had livery of the lands she held in dower, and about 1310 he was found heir to the lands of his sister Agnes or Anne. About this time he joined the Earl of Lancaster against Gaveston, and on banishment of that favourite, he was deputed, among others, to petition the king that he should be rendered incapable of holding any office. Ultimately, Gaveston, with the king's consent, surrendered at Scarborough to Pembroke, who, on the way to Wallingford, leaving him in the custody of servants, he was taken by the Earl of Warwick and led to his doom. About 1313 Pembroke was sent on a mission to Rome, and obtained a grant of lands in London, comprising the New Temple. Early in the following year, being made Warden and Lieutenant of all Scotland, till the king should go thither, he was accordingly present at the battle of Bannockburn, being stationed close by the king's bridle, and when defeat was inevitable Pembroke is said to have led him away. About 1316 he was commissioned to hold a parliament in the king's absence, and performed an active part therein. After this time he was sent to Rome on a mission to the Pontiff, but being captured on his return by a Burgundian named John de Moiller with his accomplices, he was sent to the Emperor, who obliged him to pay twenty thousand pounds of silver, on the pretence that Moiller had served the king of England without being paid his wages. About 1318 he was in the wars of Scotland, and we may suppose, on his journeys to and from the north, he regularly halted at Mitford Castle, in Northumberland, of which he was lord. Being appointed Governor of Rockingham Castle, he was constituted Guardian of the realm during the absence of the king, and held also the office of Custos of Scotland. In 1322 he fought on the king's side against Thomas of Lancaster, and was one of those who pronounced sentence of death against him at Pontefract, for which he was rewarded with the grant of several lands, chiefly in Northamptonshire.

During the following year he accompanied Isabell, Queen of England, to France, and when there he married his third wife, Mary, daughter of Guy de Chastillon, Count of St. Paul's, on which occasion he is reported to have lost his life at a tournament he gave in celebration of his nuptials, so that the bride was 'maid, wife, and widow,' in one day Dugdale, however, says he was murdered on the 23d June 1324, by reason of the part he took in the death of the Earl of Lancaster. Nicolas, on the authority of a contemporary writer, which he quotes, considers it would rather appear he died of apoplexy. His body was brought to England and buried in Westminster Abbey, where his sumptuous monument is still seen. Within the present century it had become much dilapidated, but by the means supplied by Government, and the skill of the most able artists of the time, it was restored almost to its original splendour. It is depicted both by Blore and Stothard, whose works are of great value to the historian as well as to the antiquary. Aymer de Valence was thrice married, but left no issue; first, to Beatrix, daughter of Ralph de Noel, Constable of France; secondly, to a daughter of the Earl of Barre; and thirdly, to Mary, the lady above mentioned. His said widow came to possess large estates in several counties of England, and, to her renown be it added, she was not only a bountiful benefactress to many religious houses, but became the foundress of the college of Pembroke Hall in Cambridge, an act which, Nicolas observes, 'seldom fails to ensure immortality.'

ARMS.—Barry, argent and azure, an orle of Martlets gules.

Burele de argent e de azure, od les merelos de goules.
*Roll of Arms.*

The Umfreville shield, taken from that on the effigy of an early Umfreville in Hexham Abbey church. Surtees, in his *History of Durham*, says the arms are, Gules, a cinquefoil within an orle of crosses patonce or.

## Ingram de Umfreville.

INGRAM DE UMFREVILLE, as Hodgson, the historian of Northumberland, relates, was, in all probability, brother to Gilbert de Umfreville, the first Earl of Angus, in right of his mother. He was a Scotch Baron, and comes prominently before the reader of Scottish history from 1291 to the period of the battle of Bannockburn. It is likely that another of the same name, probably his son, figures before the public from the time of the battle of Neville's Cross in 1346 down to the fiftieth year of Edward the Third, 1376.

It is accordingly the first Ingram of whom we desire to render some account. He appears, says Hodgson, 'as a luminary above the ordinary magnitude in the constellation of the eminent men of his time.' He was present at Norham, when the claims of the several candidates for the Scottish crown were arbitrated, and in the year following he witnessed John de Baliol do homage to the first Edward in the great hall of the castle in Newcastle-upon-Tyne. In 1296 he surrendered the castle of Dumbarton to the king of England, and his two daughters, Eve and Isabella, were given up as hostages of his fidelity to that monarch. In the following year King Edward summoned him to march with his whole force against the rebel subjects of Scotland, but on this occasion we have some cause to suspect he was disobedient, and may have favoured the independence of that country. In 1302, the Scots sent him to France to watch over the interest of their land in the negotiations which were about to take place. During the year afterwards, he wrote to John Comyn, Regent, and his party, a storming letter, telling how a peace had been settled between England and France without including Scotland therein, and urging them to stand out boldly and maintain the rights of their own country. In 1305, however, he had again embraced the English interest, and subsequently Edward the Second took him into favour, making him a warden in Galloway, and one of the council of Robert de Clifford. In 1308 he was defeated by Edward Bruce in that district, and on his forces being cut off, he escaped with difficulty to Butel Castle. Barbour relates that about this time Umfreville caused a red bonnet set upon a spear to be borne about wherever he went, to indicate that he had attained the height of chivalric prowess and bearing.[1]

By a writ directed by Edward the Second, in 1309, to the Sheriff of Northumberland, Ingram de Umfreville claimed twelve messuages, one hundred and twenty acres of land, eighty acres of meadow, three hundred acres of wood, and one thousand acres of pasture in Elsden, in Northumberland, as related and next of kin to Gilbert de Umfreville, then deceased. Shortly afterwards King Edward ordered his warden of Scotland to see that Umfreville was bountifully supplied for the good service rendered to his father and himself. He is styled Baron in 1310, and empowered to take into the King's allegiance such Galwegians as had been opposed to him but wished to be received into the royal favour. Afterwards he appears to have taken part with the Earl of Lancaster in accomplishing the death of Gaveston, for his name is in the list of those who received pardon for that occurrence. His reply to the King of England at Bannockburn, mentioned in the

---

[1] P. 181.

text, is the last notice we have of him, so far as the compiler has seen among the public records, in the early period of the fourteenth century.

We have no record either of his marriage or of what issue he left, but one of the same name, as has been observed, was known in public life for above fifty years after the battle of Bannockburn.

> ARMS.—In the Roll of Arms of the reign of Henry the Third the Umfreville arms are—Or, a cinquefoil gules, within a bordure azure semée of horse-shoes or. Again, when Sir Gilbert of that name married Matilda, Countess of Angus, by whom he became Earl of Angus, his arms, according to Nisbet (vol. i. p. 391), were—Azure, a cinquefoil within an orle of eight cross crosslets or. The only notice I have seen of the arms of Sir Ingram de Umfreville is in 'Documents of the History of Scotland, 1286 to 1306, selected and arranged by Joseph Stevenson, Esq. : Edinburgh, 1870, 2 vols' In vol. ii p. 12, we observe that, to a 'Promise' made by the Scottish Commissioners in France, dated Oct 22, 1295, Umfreville's seal is attached 'by a cord of green silk. It is uninjured, and a very beautiful specimen of art.' The original is deposited in the Imperial archives at Paris, S. H. S. J. 457, No. 3.

# INDEX.

AYR CASTLE taken by Bruce, 14.

BANNOCKBURN, site of the battle called Bannockmoor, 30; course of the stream, 33; bridged over after the battle by the bodies of men and horses, 107.

Baston, Robert, a Carmelite friar, 29; being captured, he wrote Latin verses on the battle, 128.

Berkeley, Maurice de, escapes from battle, 114.

Bloody Faulds, English killed there, 113.

Brabant, two knights of, expelled from the English army, and welcomed by the Scots, 73; sent home with rich gifts, 130.

Bruce, King Robert, 5; his penetrative wisdom, 9; success at Loudon Hill, 10; recognition of and declaration as king, 12; agrees with Menteith for surrender of Dumbarton Castle, 13; recovers the castles of Dumfries, Dalswinton, Ayr, and Lanark, 14; his displeasure at the agreement made by his brother Edward for surrender of Stirling Castle, 16; endeavours to increase the Scottish army, 20; his success, 21; assembles his forces at Torwood, 22; examines the route to Stirling, and fixes on Bannockmoor as the place whereon he would fight for freedom, 30; examines his army, 37; resolves his troops should meet the enemy on foot, 38; arranges for battle, 42; moves toward Bannockburn, 43; orders pits to be dug at the Roman way near Milton, 43; examines them, 47; draws up his force on Bannockmoor, 48; issues a proclamation that each fainthearted man might go home, 48; sends the servants and stores to a valley on Gillies' Hill, 50; appoints Randolph to prevent the English passing near St. Ninians, 51; sends Douglas and Keith Marshal to observe the approach of the enemy, 51; occupies Coxet Hill, 53; detects the advance of Clifford and reminds Randolph of his charge, 54; agrees that Douglas may assist Randolph, 58; marshals his troops in the field, 61; kills Sir Henry Bohun, 62; reminds his chief men how the battle should be fought, 67-71; confers knighthood on several of his leaders, 78; slightly alters his original plan of battle, 80; sends Keith Marshal to disperse the English archers, 95; leads his own division into battle, 98; raises his war-cry, and the Scots overcome the enemy, 107; consents that Douglas pursue King Edward, 109; receives Sir Marmaduke Twenge as prisoner, 123; orders the dead to be buried, 125; deals out most liberally the spoil of the English, 130.

Bruce, Sir Edward, 6; captures the castles of Rutherglen and Dundee, 15; foolishly arranges with Sir Philip Mowbray for the surrender of Stirling Castle, 16; his reply to his brother, the king, 17; arrives with his troops at Torwood, 22; is appointed to the charge of the right wing of the army, 40; forms with his warriors upon high ground the van of the Scots, 80; his division first encountered by the enemy, 89; resists the onset nobly, 101; sent by the king to capture Bothwell Castle, 126.

CLIFFORD, SIR ROBERT, sent by King Edward with cavalry to relieve Stirling Castle, 53; gives battle to Randolph, 55; defeated, 64; his body found among the slain at Bannockburn, 122.

DALSWINTON CASTLE, taken by Bruce, 14.

De Argentine, Sir Giles, placed on one side of King Edward's bridle at Bannockburn, 83; quits the field with the king, and on returning is slain, 109.

Douglas, James, 6; captures the strong castle of Roxburgh, 15; assembles his followers at Torwood, 22; appointed with the Steward to command the left wing of the army, 41; sent with Keith Marshal to observe the English, 51; advances to the assistance of Randolph, 58; receives the honour of knighthood, 78; enters into battle, 93; presses the enemy most severely, 102; asks the Bruce for leave to pursue King Edward, 111; chases him, 116.

Dumfries Castle won by Bruce, 15.

Dundee Castle taken by Edward Bruce, 15.

EDINBURGH CASTLE captured by Randolph, 15.

Edward II. proposes to invade Scotland, 17; sends for troops from Gascony and Flanders, and desires the Earl of Ulster and others to assist him, 18; arrives at Newminster Abbey, 19; appoints John Duke of Argyle High Admiral of the western fleet of England, 20; proceeds to Berwick, and thence to Edinburgh, 22; his large army, 25; pomp and magnificence of, 26; expects Scotland to be taken and divided among his people, 29; pauses, probably on obtaining a sight of Stirling Castle, 61; places the Earl of Pembroke on one side of his bridle and De Argentine on the other, 83; orders the trumpet to sound for battle, 86; his agonising feelings on being defeated, 108; quits the field and rides to Stirling Castle, 110; Mowbray advises him to depart, and he proceeds towards Linlithgow, 111; Douglas pursues him, 116; he reaches the Castle of Dunbar, and is received by the Earl of March, 117; is conveyed in a boat to England, 118.

English army, great dependence placed on the cavalry, 8; knights and men-at-arms considered invincible, 9; splendid appearance of, 27, 51; van led by Gloucester and Hereford, 89; archers wing their shafts most fatally on the Scots, 91; attacked by Keith Marshal and dispersed, 96; both cavalry and infantry driven back by the Scots, 103; whole battalions quit the field on being defeated, 112; numbers who fell and were made prisoners, 121.

GILLIES' HILL, servants sent thither, 50; they advance downward to battle, 104.

Gloucester, Earl of, leads with Hereford the van of the English army, 61; attacks the division under Sir Edward Bruce, 89; attempts in defeat to turn the tide of battle, and is slain, 106; his body sent to King Edward at Berwick, 114.

HEREFORD, EARL OF, in the van of the English army, 61; joins Gloucester in attacking Sir Edward Bruce, 89; on defeat of the English escapes to Bothwell Castle, 114; delivered up to Bruce, 126; exchanged for five illustrious prisoners, 127.

ISLE OF MAN conquered by Bruce, 16.

KEITH, SIR ROBERT, Earl Marshal, sent with Douglas to reconnoitre the English, 51; his troop of horse accompanies Randolph to encounter Clifford, 55; attacks the English archers and disperses them, 96; immense slaughter of the English by his cavalry, 105.

LANARK CASTLE taken by Bruce, 14.

Linlithgow Castle captured by William Binnock and others, 14.

MARCH, PATRICK, EARL OF, receives King Edward into his castle of Dunbar, 117; takes from him a release of his service, and gets him conveyed in a boat to England, 118.

Mauley, Edward de, found drowned in Bannockburn, 122.

# INDEX. 187

Maurice, Abbot of Inchaffray, performs mass before the Scottish army, 77 ; admonishes the warriors therein to perform their duty in delivering the land from bondage, 85.

Menteith, Sir John, treacherously agrees to deliver up to Bruce the fortress of Dumbarton, 13 ; liberated from prison, 21 ; fights at Bannockburn, and is liberally rewarded, 125.

Milton, deep pits dug near, by order of Bruce, 43.

Moray, Thomas Randolph, Earl of, takes the Castle of Edinburgh, 15 ; comes with his followers to Torwood, 22 ; appointed a leader in the army, 40 ; set to prevent the English reaching Stirling, 51 ; attacked by Sir Robert Clifford, 55 ; overcomes him, 64 ; his division enters into battle, 91 ; maintains the fight with great bravery, 102.

Mowbray, Sir Philip, stipulates with Edward Bruce to surrender Stirling Castle, and the agreement disapproved of by Bruce, 16 ; goes to London and informs King Edward of what he had done, 17 ; on the king's defeat advises him to proceed to England, 111 ; yields the castle to Bruce, and enters his service, 124.

NEW PARK, its position, 30 ; a hunting field for the Scottish kings, 31 ; the battle fought within its limits, 32.

Northburge, Roger de, keeper of the king's signet, captured with his two clerks, 124.

O'CONNOR, Eth, and other Irish chiefs, summoned by Edward to assist in subduing Bruce, 18.

PEMBROKE, Aymer de Valence, Earl of, defeated at London Hill, 10 ; appointed Governor of Scotland, 18 ; stationed on one side of the king's bridle before battle, 88.

Perth invested and taken by Bruce, 14.

ROMAN road crossed the Bannock near Milton, 33.

Roxburgh Castle taken by Douglas, 15.

Rutherglen Castle won by Edward Bruce, 15.

SAINT FILLAN, the miraculous arm of, 72.

Scott, Michael, inventor of the iron skull-cap, 6.

Scottish army, number of, previous to battle, 36 ; four divisions of, each under its respective leader, 40, 41 ; moves forward to New Park, 42 ; localities occupied by, 45 ; mass celebrated before it, 46 ; position of, when the battle commenced, 78-81 ; moves onward while fighting with the enemy, 96 ; always maintains its position in proper line, 103 ; assisted by the camp-followers from Gillies' Hill, 104 ; cavalry perform an important movement, 105 ; ultimately victorious, 107 ; loss in battle, 122.

Seton, Alexander, deserts from the English, 73.

Steward, Walter the, arrives with his followers at Torwood, 22 ; unites with Douglas in commanding the left wing of the army, 41 ; is knighted by the king, 78 ; stationed for battle, 80 ; enters into conflict, 93 ; presses the enemy most severely, 102.

Stirling Castle, Sir Philip Mowbray agrees to surrender it if not relieved by midsummer 1314, 16 ; situation of it, 32 ; King Edward being defeated flies thither, 110 ; fugitives flock to the crags near it, 113 ; surrendered to Bruce, 124.

TWENGE, SIR MARMADUKE, renders himself to Bruce, and is sent home free of ransom, 123.

WINCHBURGH, where the English in flight feed their horses, 117.

ULSTER, RICHARD DE BURG, Earl of, invited with his forces to assist King Edward against Bruce, 18.

Umfreville, Sir Ingram de, asked by King Edward if the Scots would fight, 83 ; his reply on seeing them kneel in the act of devotion, 86.

*By the same Author.*

## HISTORY OF THE BATTLE OF OTTERBURN, FOUGHT IN 1388,

With Map, etc., and Memoirs of the Warriors who engaged in that conflict. Crown 8vo.

London, Edinburgh, and Newcastle-upon-Tyne, 1857.

---

## POEMS:

Including Tales, Ballads, and Songs,

With Portrait. Foolscap 8vo.

Kelso, 1867.

"Turning to 'Poems' by Robert White, we come at last to some really genuine poetic utterances. Many of the subjects which Mr. White selects to sing are original, and some exceedingly beautiful. There is not the least affectation in his verses, and yet there is a certain polish and grace about them that lead us to believe great care has been bestowed on their composition. Above all, we admire his simplicity, and the pathos that grows out of this simplicity."—*London Review.*

"The fervid nationality of Mr. White's muse would of itself recommend his poems to all sons of Scotland. Patriotism glows in almost every page of the volume; the history, traditions, customs, and scenery of his native land he celebrates in song with unwearying enthusiasm. His style is fluent, graceful, and tasteful."—*Scotsman.*

---

## THE BATTLE OF NEVILLE'S CROSS, 1346;

AND

## THE BATTLE OF FLODDEN, 1513;

Contributed to Vols. i. and iii. of 'Archæologia Æliana,' new series, 1857 and 1859.

LIBRARY
JAN
13
1981

Printed in the USA
CPSIA information can be obtained
at www.ICGtesting.com
CBHW081105070624
9707CB00040B/445

9 781017 209310